MOON

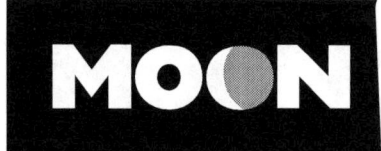

GALÁPAGOS ISLANDS

JULIAN SMITH & JEAN BROWN

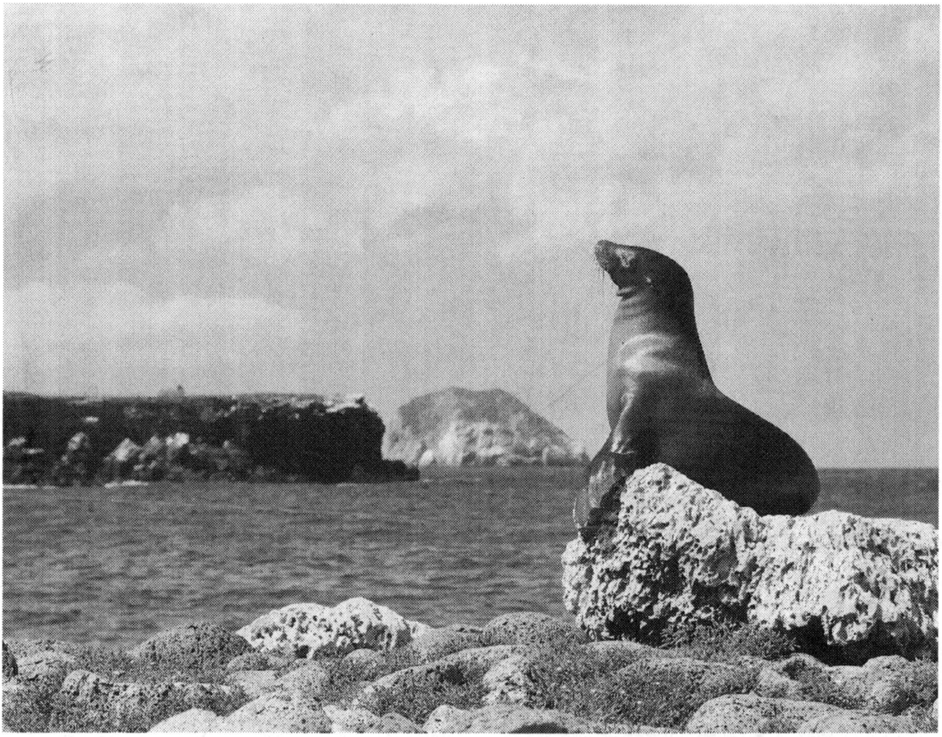

Contents

GALÁPAGOS ISLANDS

THE GALÁPAGOS ISLANDS

You don't often come across a place that's unique in the world. All too many "must-sees," no matter how glowingly they're described by guidebooks and friends, seem to pale in the harsh light of reality. But the Galápagos Islands exist truly without parallel, and I have yet to meet a disappointed visitor. Huddled far out in the Pacific Ocean, the archipelago protects a bubble of life like nowhere else on earth.

Initial impressions of the islands certainly don't promise much—the bleak, plant-stubbled landscape carries all the impact of a cheap movie set at first glance. But within a day or two of beginning your tour, you'll see things you'd never have believed existed: tortoises the size of armchairs, iguanas that swim, and birds with huge blue feet that are all completely nonplussed by your presence. By the end of your stay, you'll have gotten a taste of what the earth was like well before the human race showed up and started throwing its weight around. You'll go home understanding how a short visit to the islands more than a century ago sparked one of the greatest scientific insights in history.

Galápagos wildlife is often described as tame, but I disagree. It's not that the animals are tame, it's that they just don't care that you're there. In a self-enclosed world that has existed for millennia with no major predators, human beings are still just another large, curious-looking thing, about as threatening as a tree. The feeling of looking at acres of wild animals that don't flee at your arrival—a place where you actually have to be careful not to step on anyone as you walk down the trail—is nothing short of amazing.

HIGHLIGHTS

🄲 **Charles Darwin Research Center:** Researchers at the research station in Puerto Ayora are working to help giant tortoises – including the infamous Lonesome George – to survive (page 48).

🄲 **Punta Espinosa:** On Fernandina Island, watch flightless cormorants dry their useless wings in the sun near more marine iguanas than you'll ever see anywhere else (page 64).

🄲 **Post Office Bay:** On Floreana Island, leave a postcard in the barrel like a whaler of yore, and see if some kind stranger delivers it in person – and vice versa (page 66).

🄲 **Punta Suárez:** Waved albatrosses and an abundance of boobies are the highlights of this spot on Española Island, one of the islands' best visitors' sites (page 68).

🄲 **Wolf and Darwin Islands:** These far-off islands are known as one of the best dive spots in the world (page 69).

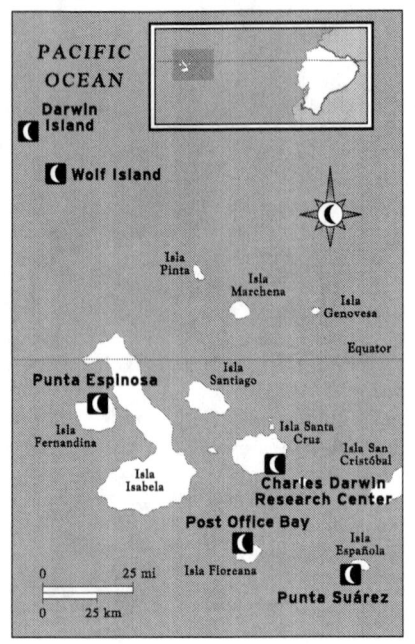

LOOK FOR 🄲 TO FIND RECOMMENDED SIGHTS, ACTIVITIES, DINING, AND LODGING.

You'll hear the Galápagos described as a "laboratory of evolution," which, along with all the other talk about species, adaptations, and 19th-century naturalists, is enough to make any nonscientist's head spin. What's going on? In a nutshell, the archipelago is as close to a perfect laboratory experiment on evolution as any place ever discovered. Nobel laureates couldn't have designed a better test if they tried—take a few species, stick them out in the middle of nowhere for a few million years, and see what happens. The result is many unique species, perfectly adapted to their difficult environment, and a few only halfway through the evolutionary process thrown in for good measure.

In part because of how special they are, the Galápagos Islands face a host of problems that threaten its singular ecosystems. The causes are nothing new—human overcrowding, exploitation of resources, too many tourists "loving" the islands to death—but the results could be tragic. If you're interested in helping, tax-deductible **donations** for research, conservation, and environmental education can be sent to the **Charles Darwin Foundation** (407 N. Washington Street, Ste. 105, Falls Church, VA 22046, tel. 703/538-6833, darwin@galapagos.org, www.darwinfoundation.org) or the **Galápagos Conservation Trust** (5 Derby Street, London, W1Y 7AD, tel. 44/020-7629-5049, gct@gct.org, www.gct.org).

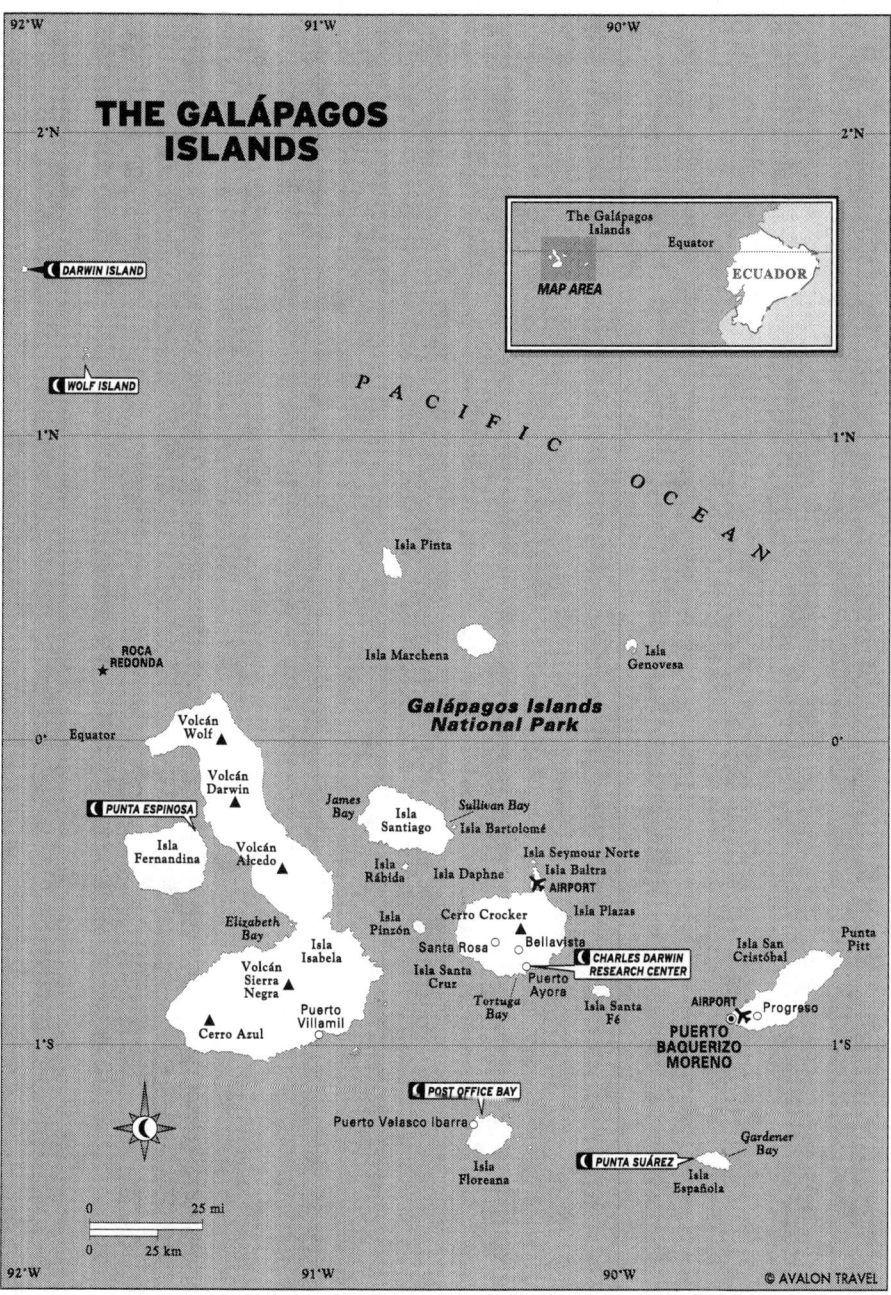

THE GALÁPAGOS ISLANDS

92°W   91°W   90°W

2°N

The Galápagos Islands
Equator
MAP AREA
ECUADOR

DARWIN ISLAND

WOLF ISLAND

PACIFIC

1°N

OCEAN

Isla Pinta

ROCA REDONDA

Isla Marchena

Isla Genovesa

Galápagos Islands
National Park

Volcán Wolf

Equator   0°

Volcán Darwin

PUNTA ESPINOSA

James Bay   Isla Santiago   Sullivan Bay
Isla Bartolomé

Isla Fernandina

Volcán Alcedo

Isla Rábida   Isla Daphne

Isla Seymour Norte
Isla Baltra
AIRPORT

Elizabeth Bay

Isla Isabela

Isla Pinzón   Cerro Crocker   Isla Plazas

Santa Rosa   Bellavista

Isla San Cristóbal   Punta Pitt

Volcán Sierra Negra

Isla Santa Cruz   Puerto Ayora

CHARLES DARWIN RESEARCH CENTER

Cerro Azul

Puerto Villamil

Tortuga Bay   Isla Santa Fé

AIRPORT   Progreso

PUERTO BAQUERIZO MORENO

1°S

POST OFFICE BAY

Puerto Velasco Ibarra

Gardener Bay

PUNTA SUÁREZ

Isla Floreana

Isla Española

0   25 mi
0   25 km

92°W   91°W   90°W   © AVALON TRAVEL

Visiting the Islands

PLANNING YOUR TIME

Since most visitors come here on packaged tours, the idea of planning your time in the Galápagos is somewhat moot. A tour of at least five days is recommended, and eight or more is better, including a half day each way to come and go. You can also come here on your own and find a tour in the islands, or take day tours out of Puerto Ayora on Santa Cruz or Puerto Baquerizo Moreno on San Cristóbal, although this is less common. (See *Choosing a Tour* for more details.)

Almost all tours visit the **Charles Darwin Research Center** in Puerto Ayora, where giant tortoises are raised from eggs, and Lonesome George may have finally found a mate. On Floreana, whose history could (and has) filled a book, check if any postcards in the barrel in **Post Office Bay** are heading in the direction of your hometown; if they are, tradition says to deliver them in person.

Punta Suárez on Española Island boasts both "Boobieville"—that would be the birds— and one of the two waved albatross breeding sites in the world. Experienced divers must not miss the underwater menagerie at **Wolf and Darwin Islands,** northwest of the main group. The largest colony of marine iguanas in the islands awaits at **Punta Espinosa** on Fernandina, next to the scraggly nests of flightless cormorants.

WHEN TO GO

High tourist season in the Galápagos occurs near the winter holidays (December–January) and during the northern hemisphere's summer (June–August). In those months, it can be hard to find space on a tour unless you book well ahead. Then again, fewer boats operate during the off-season, which can make spots scarce as well. Many boats are dry-docked for repairs and maintenance during September and October.

As far as weather is concerned, during the dry season (June–November) the islands become

ISLAND NAMES

Almost every island in the Galápagos boasts at least two names, and some have three or more, including English, Spanish, and nicknames. I've followed the lead of Michael Jackson (the author, not the singer) in selecting the names used in this book, listed here alphabetically and followed by any variations. All names are official, except Floreana and Santiago, whose official names follow in boldface.

- Baltra (South Seymour)
- Bartolomé (Bartholomew)
- Beagle
- Cowley
- Darwin (Culpepper)
- Enderby
- Española (Hood)
- Fernandina (Narborough)
- Floreana (**Santa María;** Charles)
- Genovesa (Tower)
- Isabela (Albemarle)
- Marchena (Bindloe)
- Pinta (Abingdon)
- Pinzón (Duncan)
- Plazas
- Rábida (Jervis)
- San Cristóbal (Chatham)
- Santa Cruz (Indefatigable)
- Santa Fé (Barrington)
- Santiago (**San Salvador;** James)
- Seymour Norte (North Seymour)
- Sin Nombre (Nameless)
- Tortuga (Brattle)
- Wolf (Wenman)

brown and sere as dormant vegetation waits for the rains. Skies are often cloudy but little rain falls, and the water is somewhat colder for swimming. Rains come during the wet season (January–April), alternating with hot and sunny days. The islands turn green, and sea turtles lay their eggs. November and April may well be the best overall months to visit—not too hot or cold, and not too many tourists.

The Galápagos are one hour behind mainland Ecuador (six hours behind GMT).

WHAT TO BRING

Aside from shorts and T-shirts, bring a light jacket or sweater and a pair of long pants for chilly mornings and evenings, plus a rain jacket for visiting the damp highlands. Sturdy boots are essential for the rough lava, and a hat and sunglasses keep the impact of the equatorial glare to a minimum. Bring a water bottle and refill it onboard with boiled or purified water. Sunblock and seasickness pills or wristbands should go in with your toiletries. The latter is crucial if you're prone to motion sickness; the open waters between the islands can be surprisingly rough, especially in smaller boats, although trips are rarely canceled because passengers can't stand the constant nausea. A day pack and water bottle make shore visits easier, and a bathing suit and good snorkeling equipment guarantee that you won't be caught with your trunks down in the water.

If you have any money left after booking your tour, spend it on photography equipment. Even if you're only a casual photographer, you'll feel like a pro in this wildlife photographer's nirvana. Grab close-ups with a telephoto lens—at least 200 mm, preferably 300 or even larger—and bring UV and polarizing filters to help cut the midday glare. Water protection for your gear, even if only sturdy freezer bags, is a must for *panga* rides. Finally, bring twice as much film or digital memory as you think you'll need, and then some more on top of that. You'll be amazed how quickly frames fly by, and film prices on ships and in the islands are ridiculously high.

GETTING THERE

Transport to the islands is not generally included in the coast of a tour. **TAME** and **Aerogal** both have two daily flights from Quito to Baltra for Santa Cruz via Guayaquil, leaving Quito between 7:30 and 9:30 A.M. The trip costs $407 pp round-trip (slightly less in the low seasons, May–mid-June and mid-September–end of October), and round-trip fares from Guayaquil are around $50 lower. Both carriers also operate flights to San Cristobal daily, with two flights on Sunday between 9–9:45 A.M. for the same prices. Discounts are available during high season for students with ISIC cards, available only in person on weekdays at least one day before departure at the central TAME office in Quito. Check-in is at least 90 minutes before departure. The flight takes about three hours from Quito, and you're allowed to bring one main piece of luggage up to 45 pounds.

If you booked your flight independently, make sure you're flying to the correct island at the correct time to begin your tour *before* booking your boat trip. The ticket counter in Quito is a madhouse, with tour agents checking in large groups as everyone else jostles in line. All flights originate in Quito and stop over in Guayaquil for at least one hour, where everyone often has to get off while the fuel tanks are topped off. Tours should reconfirm for you both ways—don't duplicate the reservation yourself, or the computer will erase you. If you wish, you can check a few days before departure and make sure your name is on the passenger list, not the waiting list *(lista de espera)*.

The **National Park entrance fee** is $100 pp for foreigners, payable in cash only at the airport upon arrival. Keep your receipt, because your boat captain will need to record it. The new migratory control card costs $10 and is for Ecuadorians and visitors alike. Don't loose it—you'll need to surrender it upon departure.

Tour groups are met at both airports by smiling, sign-waving guides who will direct you to the bus to take you to the dock and your waiting boat. If you're arriving without being booked on a tour, getting from Baltra to Puerto Ayora is a bit more complicated. The journey has three stages: a free bus ride to the Itabaca canal between Baltra and Santa Cruz (don't take the bus to the "muelle"), a short ferry across the channel, and another bus up and over the Santa Cruz highlands and down to Puerto Ayora. The whole trip takes about 1.5 hours. To get back to the airport from town, catch a taxi ($1) to the bus terminal on the edge of town in the morning. (The Baquerizo Moreno airport on San Cristobal is within walking or taxi distance of town.)

CHOOSING A TOUR

The only way to visit the Galápagos is by boat with a tour group; beyond that, your choices are limited to what kind of boat and, for some, whether to sleep aboard or not. Prices vary widely, as does service: When shopping around for a tour, remember that in the Galápagos—perhaps more than most destinations—you get what you pay for. Visiting the Galápagos is probably the most expensive thing you'll do in Ecuador, but if you plan it right and luck out with good weather, a good guide, and friendly companions, it can easily be one of the most amazing things you ever do.

Tour boats are organized into five classes—economic, tourist, tourist superior, first, and luxury—and trips range four–eight days, with occasional special charters of 11 and 15 days. Unless you're really strapped for cash or time, five days should be the minimum length of time you consider. Prices range from less than $750 pp for a five-day economy-class trip to $5,000 for eight days on a luxury-class vessel. (Arrival and departure days are counted as tour days.) It may lessen the sting to know that these prices include food, accommodations, transfers to and from your boat, trained guides, and all your shore visits. You'll have to pay extra for airfare to and from the islands, insurance, gratuities, souvenirs, and alcoholic or soft drinks on board.

Itineraries are strictly controlled by the National Park Service to regulate the impact of visitors on the delicate sites. This means sticking to a tight schedule, so if you sometimes feel as if you're being herded, well, you are—in theory, for the good of the islands. The only valid reasons on most boats for altering an itinerary are medical emergencies and bad weather.

Economy Boats

Prices for boats in the economic class range $1,000–1,250 pp per week, or a little less for special last-minute deals and tours that spend the nights ashore. Guides are usually not as well trained as those on luxury boats, and accommodations and food may likewise be underwhelming. Because most economy boats are small (8–16 passengers), you'll get to know your fellow travelers well—perhaps too well—and your boat will toss more on rough seas.

Certain security measures should be heeded for any economy boat tour in the Galápagos (or Ecuador, for that matter). Be sure the boat has adequate safety equipment: fire extinguishers, life jackets, and flares.

Economy-class boats, on the whole, are the best (or only) option for those on a limited budget or time frame. If you plan well and negotiate your dollars and days carefully, your trip can turn out great—even a bit of an adventure.

Moderately Priced Boats

Tourist-class and tourist superior–class boats are the most common in the islands. They're usually medium-size sailboats or motorboats holding 10–16 passengers. Accommodations are a step up from economy class, but the cabins in most are still small, with bunk beds, and the toilets are pumped by hand. Some would argue that the food in tourist class is the best, because the cooks are generally excellent and only have to cook for a small group. Guides range from mediocre to outstanding—generally, the better the boat, the better the guide.

Tourist Superior boats frequently include Genovesa in their itinerary.

Costs range $1,300–1,550 pp per week for tourist class and $1,600–1,950 pp per week for tourist superior class.

First-Class Boats

Not all but most first-class boats include a visit to the western islands of Isabela and Fernandina. These destinations are confined to the better class of boats, which can sail faster, having larger engines and fuel tanks. Most of these boats take 16–26 passengers, accommodated in comfortable cabins or staterooms with beds rather than bunks. Several are beautifully maintained sailing ships (don't expect to sail to the longer overnight destinations) and all have guides with a reputation for excellence. Prices here range $2,000–3,800 pp for a week.

Luxury Tours and Cruise Ships

If your tastes run to crisp linens and mimosas in the morning, reserve a berth on a luxury liner like the 292-foot *Celebrity Xpedition*. Boats in this class maintain a standard of luxury matching the finest hotels on the mainland. Cabins, food, and service are all top-notch, and accoutrements include things like exercise rooms, spas, and salons. For guests of Lindblad Expeditions' 47-passenger *Islander,* massages are administered on a floating, glass-bottomed pontoon in a secluded cove.

Everything is organized by loudspeaker announcement, from shore visits to buffet lunches and sit-down dinners. Guides are the cream of the crop—multilingual fluency and university degrees are the norm. Since there are several guides, groups can be split up to match guests with similar interests and energy levels. Because these boats are the largest ones plying the archipelago, they're able to visit far islands like Fernandina, Isabela, and Espanola, which lie beyond the range of smaller, slower boats. Sea rolling is minimized, although still a factor.

The short list of minuses includes a lack of intimacy with all the passengers (you can't meet them all in eight days). Everything is planned to the minute, and flexibility is restricted to the options of "go" or "not go" for any visit or landing. Luxury-class tours start at $3,800 pp per week and climb to around $5,000.

Shore-Based Tours

Those especially troubled by seasickness may be glad to hear that a few options allow you to sleep on shore. However remember that time will be wasted traveling to and from the islands every day (on smaller boats that do roll with the ocean), and many of the farther islands will remain completely out of reach. Budget travelers can find accommodations in Puerto Ayora or Baquerizo Moreno and arrange a string of day tours.

Guides

Next to a boat that doesn't sink, a good guide is the most important factor in your visit. All Galápagos guides are trained and licensed by the National Park Service. They qualify in one of three classes, in ascending order of quality: Class One, usually on economy boats or handling land-based tours; Class Two, on tourist- and tourist superior–class boats; and Class Three, on first-class and luxury boats. All guides are supposed to speak at least two languages, but Class One guides often speak little besides Spanish. Every guide has to pass rigorous examinations every three years and complete a training course on the islands every six years to keep his or her certification.

When booking a tour, ask about your guide's specific qualifications and what language he or she speaks. In general, the more expensive the tour, the better the guide.

Booking and Payment

Tours can be arranged by phone from your kitchen table in your home country, but keep in mind that the farther from the boat you set things up, the more you're paying for legwork you could conceivably do yourself. To book a cruise from abroad, a deposit of at least $200 pp (via wire transfer or Western Union) is required. Ecuador does not permit the use of credit cards for any payments by Internet or telephone, so these can't be used without the owner, the card, and the passport being present in Ecuador. Even so, only a handful of boats accept credit cards for payment in person, and these still require partial payment in cash or travelers' checks. You can pay for your flights with credit cards, albeit only when there is at least one full working day between purchase and departure.

Many travel agencies in Quito advertise tours, so shopping around is the way to go. The best deals often come when agencies are desperate to fill the last few spaces on a tour, so some judicious holding out may help save you 5–50 percent—although it could leave you stranded as well. (The best last-minute deals are on the better classes of boats.) Beyond the list included here, Safari Tours in Quito and the South American Explorers are the best sources for up-to-date information on recommended boats. Deposits range 10–50 percent, depending on the boat and tour operator. You are normally required to have paid in full 30 days before sailing, unless you're getting a last-minute deal.

Puerto Ayora is the place to go for booking a tour in the Galápagos, although this applies mainly to budget tours and not in busy season. While you're negotiating the price and itinerary, keep a few things in mind: Try not to include sites you could visit yourself, like the Darwin Center and the Santa Cruz highlands, and be sure to get the entire agreement down on paper—vouchers provided by the boat companies normally have the itineraries preprinted on them. Direct all complaints concerning tours, before or after, to the port captain (Capitanía del Puerto) if you booked in the islands, and to the agency directly if you booked in Quito or outside the country.

LIFE ON BOARD
Daily Routine
The day of arrival in the islands, you'll be shown to your boat and cabin. Don't worry if it's small (and most are, except on the cruise ships); you'll have something to keep you busy during most of the day, and any spare minutes you have, you'll probably want to spend on deck or socializing in the common area/dining room. Your guide will introduce him or herself and the rest of the crew and spend a few minutes explaining the park rules, your itinerary, and the day-to-day schedule during your stay.

Every day after that, you'll be rousted out of bed at 6 or 7 A.M. to find breakfast waiting. Chances are the boat will be in a different location—maybe even a different island—than when you went to bed, after sailing or motoring most of the night. The morning visit takes two–three hours, including the *panga* ride to shore. Your guide will direct the group along the path or down the beach, explaining what you're seeing and filling in relevant natural history details as you go.

If your guide seems overly concerned about keeping the group together and making everyone stick to the trail, try not to let it bother you. After all, these people herd thousands of tourists a year past the same sites, and a surprising number of folks think that, because they paid so much money to come here, they shouldn't have to follow orders once they arrive. This is simply not true. Better too strict than too lax, for the sake of the islands. The same sentiment applies when your guides insist that you wear a lifejacket during *panga* rides; they face fines and jail time if they're caught with passengers not wearing one.

Back on board, you'll find your cabin clean and lunch ready. The midday meal is casual—a buffet on cruise ships and fixed menus on smaller vessels. Your guide will announce the departure time for the afternoon excursion. There's usually time for a short break of an hour or so to rest, digest, or update your journal. Occasionally, the boat will travel between sites by day.

The afternoon visit runs much like the morning, except now the best light for photos comes with the setting sun. If you have the opportunity to **snorkel**, don't miss it. Where else can you swim with sea lions and turtles, along with the usual gorgeous fish and marine life? Wetsuits are handy, especially in the cold season, but not necessary in the warm season; wearing just a swimsuit, most people can last about half an hour in the water before getting chilled.

There should be some time before dinner to wash up and relax. Dinner is the most significant meal of the day; on cruise ships, it's a formal, sit-down affair with invitations to the captain's table and all that jazz. Your crew might surprise you with fresh lobster or fish, such as *pargo* (red snapper) or *bacalao* (cod). After the meal, your guide will give a talk on what you saw today and where you'll be visiting tomorrow.

An evening's post-dinner entertainment ranges from dancing on cruise ships to swapping tall tales over beers on sailboats. Remember that drinks are not included in the tour price, so be ready to pay the piper the day of departure. A day in the equatorial sun takes a lot out of you, though, so don't be embarrassed to make a beeline from the dinner table to bed.

Tipping

Giving a gratuity at the end of the voyage is customary and should be factored into the cost of your Galápagos trip. Your crew and guide work hard, as they'll probably remind you—beyond that, any tip should reflect the level of service, so use your best judgment. Cash and travelers' checks are both welcome. The usual procedure is to tip the guide separately from the rest of the crew. Crew tipping should be done through a tip box or given to the entire group at once to minimize the chances of anyone getting short-changed. As an example, on the tourist and tourist superior boats, the average tip is around 5 percent of the cost of the cruise; on the first-class and luxury boats, 10 percent is more normal, with the total divided between crew and guide.

Safety and Annoyances

All this talk of natural history seems to fuel some biological urge to breed, or at least try to, since complaints of male guides hitting on female passengers are so common. If an island tryst wasn't in your plans, decline politely, and if it persists, report him to the tour operator.

Smoking is prohibited on any of the uninhabited islands and at all the visitors sites on the inhabited islands. Most boats have no-smoking policies as well.

DIVING IN THE GALÁPAGOS

You must be getting tired of superlatives by now, but heed at least one more: The Galápagos are among the most spectacular dive destinations in the world. The islands' underwater riches have been known since the New York Zoological Society's Oceanographic Expedition sent divers with lead boots and hand-pumped air hoses in 1925. In 1998, the long-awaited Special Law for the Galápagos extended the protected marine zone to 40 nautical miles from the shores of the islands. At last count, there were more than 60 marine visitor sites throughout the archipelago, many on islands closed to visitors above the surface.

Diving in the Galápagos is not for beginners. Cold waters make a wetsuit essential, and the best marine life usually keeps to areas of strong currents—up to 3.5 knots in places. Visibility is poor, ranging 10–25 meters (half that of the Caribbean). Many dives are in open water, making holding onto coral not only permitted, but essential. Luckily, there is a decompression chamber in Puerto Ayora.

If you have the necessary skills, though, the Galápagos Islands offer a world-class diving experience, with schools of fish so thick that the water seems alive. Sea jacks arrive in boisterous groups, while cod wait farther down. Active volcanic vents keep things interesting, but not nearly as much as a school of sharks circling in a tornado of teeth. The list goes on from there: whale sharks, manta rays, sperm whales, marine iguanas, and penguins all make appearances, and the animals below the surface are as approachable as those on land.

Live-aboard charters are the usual way to go. Most large Galápagos tour agencies can book dive trips aboard the small number of boats that are equipped for it. Many companies require a certain level of experience: an open water certification and a minimum number of dives (usually 25), and sometimes a medical certificate.

The best diving is during the hot season (roughly December–May), with water temperatures 20–25°C, making a three-millimeter wetsuit adequate. Temperatures drop to 15°C in the cold season, when a six-millimeter wetsuit with hood, booties, and gloves becomes necessary. Other than your own wetsuit, you'll also want to bring a mask, dive alert whistle, and sausage or scuba tuba. Boats supply tanks, air, and weights. You can rent gear at Galápagos Sub-Aqua or Scuba Iguana in Puerto Ayora, but since tours go straight to the boat from the airport, this can be complicated.

A full day's sail north of the main island group, the **Wolf** and **Darwin Islands** aren't even on most maps of the Galápagos. But they should be, because the diving here is some of the best on the planet. Schools of hundreds of hammerheads can be seen off Wolf, and gigantic whale sharks cruise slowly by between June and November. Bottlenose dolphins are common at Darwin's Arch.

Day dive trips are available through several agencies in Puerto Ayora to nearby dive sites, including Academy Bay, Santa Fe, Gordon Rocks, Daphne Minor, Mosquera Islet, Seymour, and Cousins. Occasional dives from the regular cruise boats have been outlawed with the introduction of tighter park regulations in 2007.

Because most visitors depart by plane, plan on leaving a day free at the end of your dive trip to avoid possible pressurization problems. (Most dive tours spend the last day on Santa Cruz.)

Dive Agencies

Fernando Zambrano of **Galápagos Sub-Aqua** (tel. 4/230-5514 or 4/230-5507 in Guayaquil, tel. 5/252-6350 or 5/252-6633 in Puerto Ayora,

www.galapagos-sub-aqua.com) was the first scuba guide on the islands and boasts two decades of diving experience. His outfit has a good safety record. Eight-day live-aboard trips are $3,000–4,500 pp. They also have an office in Puerto Ayora, where they offer day dives for $100–160 pp per day.

Also in Puerto Ayora is **Scuba Iguana** (tel. 5/252-6497, info@scubaiguana.com, www .scubaiguana.com), run by dive master Matias Espinosa, who was featured in the *Galápagos* IMAX movie. Daily dive prices start at $100 pp for two dives in Academy Bay and rise to $160 pp for other destinations. They also book live-aboards.

The **Aggressors I & II** (www.aggressors .com) operate top-of-the-line dives to Darwin and Wolf. Prices start around $3,800 pp, rising to $4,700 pp for a week.

HISTORY

The Galápagos Islands' inhospitable nature has saved them for much of their history. In the middle of the ocean, with hardly a drop of fresh water, the islands left visitors unimpressed for centuries before permanent settlers managed to scrape a toehold in the volcanic soil. The world eventually became aware of the treasure secreted among the barren-looking islands, just as early visitors were beginning to permanently alter the islands' natural balance.

Early Visitors

Pre-Inca *indígenas* from the coast of Ecuador were probably the first to visit the islands, as evidenced by fish bones and food remains uncovered in various spots. Blown out to sea by storms and swept west by the Humboldt Current, these hapless sailors often made one-way journeys of discovery. In 1572, the Spanish chronicler Miguel Sarmiento de Gamboa reported that the Inca Tupac Yupanqui had visited the archipelago on the advice of a seer who flew ahead to scout the way. However, this account is generally considered a legend, since the Incas weren't seagoing people.

In 1535, a ship carrying Tomás de Berlanga,

Bishop of Panama, stood becalmed off the coast of what would become Colombia on its way to the Spanish settlements in Peru. The Panama Current pushed the helpless vessel southwest for weeks before washing it among the Galápagos. The thirst-maddened crew chewed cactus pads for moisture before stumbling across pools of rainwater. Setting sail once more, the ship and crew spent almost a month at sea before the Bahía de Caráquez came into sight.

In a subsequent letter to the Spanish king, Berlanga described the islands' unique and fearless wildlife, but concluded that they weren't fit for colonization. He described the giant tortoises as having shells like riding saddles (called *galápagos* in Spanish), and the description stuck. On the 1574 *Orbis Terrarum,* the map of the known world, a small cluster of dots off the South American coast bore the label *Insulae de los Galopegos.*

That same century, the Spanish conquistador Diego de Rivadeneira landed in the Galápagos after 25 days at sea. On his return to Guatemala, Rivadeneira tried to claim discovery of the islands, calling them Las Islas Encantadas (The Enchanted Islands) after their supposed tendency to drift on the ocean, coming and going in the enshrouding mist. Half a century later, English pilot Sir John Hawkins wrote: "Some fourscore leagues to the westward of the Cape lyeth a heape of Ilands the Spaniards call Illas de los Galápagos; they are desert and beare no fruite."

Pirates and Whalers

During the 17th century, Dutch, English, and French pirates turned the Galápagos into a base for attacks on coastal ports and Spanish galleons laden with treasure for Madrid. Sir Francis Drake was among the buccaneers who attacked rich port cities like Guayaquil before retreating to the islands to escape pursuers. The pirate William Ambrose Cowley made the first working map of the Galápagos, naming them after British royalty. Floreana and Santiago Islands were originally dubbed Charles and James, respectively, after British monarchs, and Isabela

was once called Albemarle after a duke of the same title.

Pirates were the first to realize that the islands' giant tortoises could be stored aboard to provide fresh meat for long voyages, a practice that was honed to deadly perfection by 18th-century whalers. In 1841, Herman Melville visited the Galápagos on one of hundreds of whaling ships plying the rich waters around the archipelago, inspiring his account entitled *Las Encantadas.* By then, it was apparent that the Galápagos were worth something, so on February 12, 1832, Ecuador beat out halfhearted attempts by the United States and Great Britain to claim the archipelago officially. ("A harmless and even comical opinion," muses Kurt Vonnegut in his novel *Galápagos,* about as significant as if the country "had annexed to its territory a passing cloud of asteroids.")

Darwin's Visit

Charles Darwin's visit aboard the H.M.S. *Beagle* in 1835 gained renown with the publication of *The Origin of Species* in 1859. Although the visit itself didn't actually give the budding naturalist an instant lightning-strike of inspiration, it did provide crucial evidence for Darwin's later theories and culture-shaking publications. (See the sidebar *Charles Darwin and the Galápagos.*)

An isolated penal colony established on Floreana in the 1830s began a proud Galápagos tradition that continued throughout the 19th and 20th centuries. The brainchild of Galápagos governor-general José Villamil, the first colony was home to Ecuadorians whose death sentences were commuted to a life of toil on the islands. Almost 300 convicts made a meager living growing a native lichen for dyes and selling produce to passing ships. Englishman Colonel J. Williams, the infamously cruel governor of the colony (1839–1841), was driven out in an uprising that left only 80 convicts behind. Other penal colonies, on San Cristóbal in the 1890s and Isabela in the 1960s, have also begun to enter the realm of legend.

CHARLES DARWIN AND THE GALÁPAGOS

The man who would make the Galápagos famous with what some have called "the greatest idea anyone has ever had, anywhere" was born in 1809 into an upper-middle-class British family. Throughout his childhood and youth, Darwin was fascinated by nature, constantly collecting specimens to study. He was thrilled to accept the post of unpaid naturalist onboard the *H.M.S. Beagle,* a small sailing vessel which left Plymouth, England, on December 27, 1831.

During the voyage, Darwin befriended Captain Robert Fitzroy, who shared his cabin and saw the young landlubber through the seasickness that plagued him the entire trip. The *Beagle* landed twice off the coast of Africa before crossing the Atlantic and beginning a two-year exploration of South America's eastern coast. Darwin roamed the forests near Bahía, Brazil, and rode alongside *gauchos* in the high plains of Uruguay. In 1834, the *Beagle* rounded Cape Horn and headed up the western coast of Chile and Peru.

Darwin had already noticed things along the way that challenged the biblical theory of creation. Dinosaur bones in Argentina and fossilized sea shells at 4,000 meters in the Andes proved to him the theories of slowly changing land masses put forth in Charles Lyell's groundbreaking *Principles of Geology.*

During a five-week stay in the Galápagos Islands, Darwin managed to visit San Cristóbal, Floreana, Santiago, and Isabela. The naturalist filled his time by collecting samples, observing the animals, and taking notes. What he discovered provided crucial clues that led to the gradual birth of the theory of evolution through natural selection. From the tortoise shells and finch beaks, shaped differently from island to island, Darwin began to ponder the idea of separate species evolving from a common ancestor. The fearlessness and beneficial adaptations of the iguanas, cormorants, and penguins all added pieces to the puzzle.

Before returning home to England, the *Beagle* crossed the Pacific and Indian Oceans, stopping at New Zealand, Australia, and

Mauritus before rounding the tip of Africa. The ship sailed into Falmouth Harbor on October 2, 1836. Darwin was never the same after the voyage. His studies took on an intensity they never had before.

When the *Beagle* set sail, Darwin was still a firm believer in the biblical story of creation and the immutability of life on earth. But after witnessing the animals on different islands, similar enough to be related but different enough to be separate species, he slowly began to change his mind.

However, it would take another two decades before Darwin was ready to publish his theories. He spent much of this time worrying about the impact his work would have on England's highly evangelical society. Further, he also could have faced criminal charges of sedition and blasphemy. In the end, only the threat of someone else publishing the theory first — which Alfred Russel Wallace was about to do in 1858 — finally spurred Darwin to act. That same year, friends arranged for Darwin and Wallace to read a joint paper to the Linnean Society of London, formally presenting evolution to the public for the first time.

On November 24, 1859, Darwin published **On the Origin of Species by Means of Natural Selection,** a work that would forever change the way we view ourselves and our place in the world. In a nutshell, the book proposed a **theory of evolution,** in which separate groups of animals change over time in response to their environment.

In the *Origin of Species,* Darwin proposed an idea so simple that it was almost sublime: that groups of organisms changed over time in response to the challenges their individual members faced every day. Perhaps gazelles hadn't always been fleet of foot — perhaps they hadn't even always been gazelles! The ability to run, along with countless other qualities, such as a long neck to reach tree leaves up high, thick fur to stay warm in winter, or a nervous disposition to make an animal bolt when danger threatened, could have developed over time in response to pressures from the surrounding world.

Perhaps, Darwin suggested, these traits – called **adaptations** – were not the whims of an almighty being, but rather the result of some spontaneous natural process that could be quantified and studied.

One germ for the idea was the Galápagos finches, which displayed a wide array of beak shapes and sizes to take advantage of different types of food, but still closely resembled each other. Darwin wondered if one sort of finch arrived at the islands long ago, then had somehow become all these different kinds in the interim.

To explain the process, Darwin proposed a mechanism called **descent with modification.** He based it on observations of animals and plants in captivity, which produced many more offspring than their environmental "niche" could possibly support. Only the ones best-suited to their environment survived to reproduce.

This idea became the cornerstone of the process of **natural selection:**

As many more individuals of each species are born than can possibly survive; and as, consequently, there is a frequently recurring struggle for existence, it follows that any being, if it vary however slightly in any manner profitable to itself, under the complex and sometimes varying conditions of life, will have a better chance of surviving, and thus be naturally selected.

If somehow these "selected" organisms could pass on the qualities that made them successful to their offspring, then the members of that particular line, logically, would eventually out-reproduce their less "fit" competitors and spread their successful selves over the landscape – hence the book's subtitle, *The Preservation of Favoured Races in the Struggle for Life.*

The process could even work in "reverse," leading to the loss of adaptations that were suddenly no longer beneficial. On an island with no predators, and hence no need to fly to safety, wings might eventually just get in the way. Birds that could somehow forgo growing them would be able to swim after fish more efficiently and have more energy left over for other things – such as reproducing – than their fellows. Thus the flightless cormorant.

Darwin was the first to admit that his theory was still full of holes, and that he was not the first to suggest this concept, having drawn on the work of a long list of scientists, including Jean-Baptiste Lamark, Charles Lyell, Thomas Malthus, and Darwin's own grandfather, Erasmus. In Darwin's words, this process of **evolution** was "clumsy, wasteful, blundering, low, and horribly cruel," characterized by inefficiency, lifelong struggle, and probable extinction – surely not the method employed by sublime Nature.

Although it's as well documented today as any phenomenon in science (and therefore to many a "fact," not a "theory"), the ideas in the *Origin of Species* caused an uproar in Victorian England, just as its author had feared. The clergy especially had a problem with it: Evolution implied that what might have once been created by God must have been in need of improvement.

But Darwin's evidence was overwhelming, and his argument fit the 19th-century spirit of exploration and discovery (and, conveniently, the contemporary attitude of more "advanced" cultures colonizing and dominating more "primitive" ones). Darwin tried his best to stay out of the furor his theory caused, preferring to leave that to other scientists, such as his friend and "bulldog," English biologist Thomas Henry Huxley. Darwin's theories gradually became accepted among scientists and the general public.

The naturalist who was now known worldwide spent the last decades of his life writing up his notes, studying plants, and living in the Downe countryside with his wife and their 10 children. He died on April 19, 1882, and was buried in honor next to Sir Isaac Newton in Westminster Abbey in London.

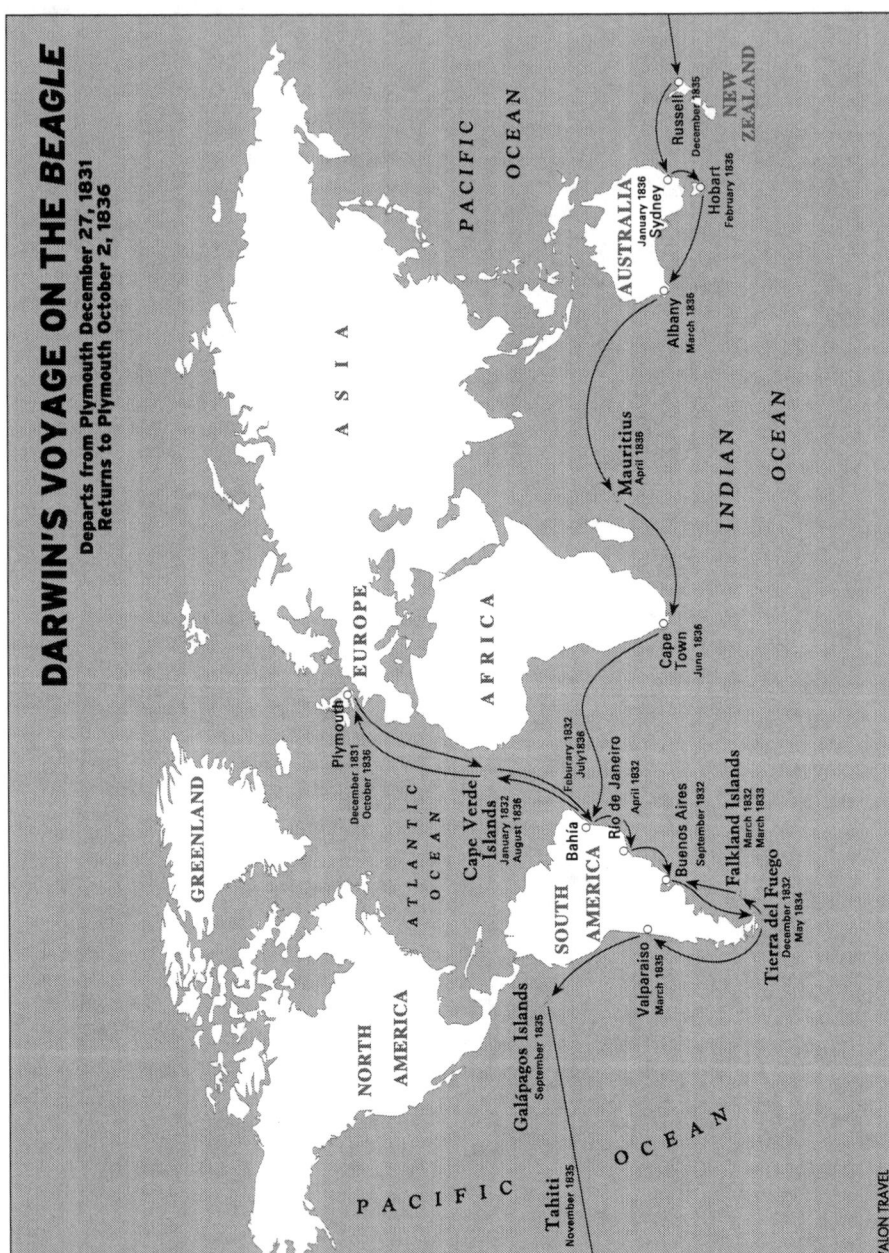

DARWIN'S VOYAGE ON THE BEAGLE

Departs from Plymouth December 27, 1831
Returns to Plymouth October 2, 1836

NORTH
AMERICA

GREENLAND

EUROPE

ASIA

AFRICA

ATLANTIC
OCEAN

PACIFIC
OCEAN

INDIAN
OCEAN

PACIFIC
OCEAN

SOUTH
AMERICA

Plymouth
December 1831
October 1836

Cape Verde
Islands
January 1832
August 1836

Bahia
Feburary 1832
July 1836

Río de Janeiro
April 1832

Buenos Aires
September 1832

Falkland Islands
March 1832
March 1833

Tierra del Fuego
December 1832
May 1834

Valparaíso
March 1835

Galápagos Islands
September 1835

Tahiti
November 1835

Cape
Town
June 1836

Mauritius
April 1836

AUSTRALIA
January 1836

Sydney

Albany
March 1836

Hobart
February 1836

Russell
December 1835

NEW
ZEALAND

© AVALON TRAVEL

First Settlers

The islands' strategic location stirred serious foreign interest during the early 20th century. The U.S. offered to lease the Galápagos to protect the entrance to the new Panama Canal, finished in 1914, and the U.S. Navy trained in the waters of the archipelago during World War I. During World War II, the Ecuadorian government allowed the U.S. Sixth Air Force to set up a station on Baltra and a few other islands to protect the Panama Canal and to monitor Japanese activity in the South Pacific. The airport built on Baltra was given to Ecuador after the war.

William Beebe's book *Galapagos: World's End,* published in 1924, helped change the public's image of the islands from a strange, forbidding place to a starkly beautiful sanctuary with a unique ecology. A healthy dose of weirdness remained, though, and seemed to attract outcasts and settlers with more fancy than practicality, especially on Floreana (see *Floreana* for more details). Norwegians arrived to catch and smoke fish, whereas others came simply for the isolation and freedom.

Recent Conservation Efforts

The islands were declared a national park in 1959. The Charles Darwin Research Center in Puerto Ayora, opened in 1964, was followed four years later by the Galápagos National Park Service, signaling the start of an earnest effort to study the islands and conserve them for the world. Tourism began in the 1930s, when wealthy boaters stopped off for a few days to paint their ships' names on the rocks and admire the giant tortoises over martinis and pâté. Metropolitan Touring began operating some exclusive tours in the 1960s. A monthly ship from Guayaquil was the only other way to

THAR SHE BLEW

When the British whaler *Rattler* began the first reconnaissance of the Galápagos in 1793, its crew quickly realized what a gold mine they had found. Between starting the Post Office barrel on Floreana and making the first workable charts of the islands, the *Rattler's* crew marveled at the pods of sperm, humpback, and fin whales on almost every horizon.

When word reached Europe and North America, the hunt began. The second whaler to visit the islands, the British ship *William,* took 42 sperm whales in 18 days – and that was just the beginning. The first half of the 19th century brought an onslaught of traffic to the islands. In addition to attracting attention for the numerous whales, the Galápagos made a perfect stopover on the way to the even richer grounds of the South Pacific Islands. The Galápagos provided a safe harbor where wood and water could be found inland.

Most important, the islands supported a seemingly endless supply of animals that did everything but hop into the pot and cook themselves. Giant tortoises in particular were almost wiped out because it was discovered that they could survive unaided for months in ships' holds, providing fresh meat well into a long ocean voyage. It became a wholesale slaughter: In nine days, the USS *Moss* took 350 tortoises, only to be outdone by the USS *Uncas,* which captured 416 in five days. More than 15,000 tortoises were taken from Floreana alone, leading to the extinction of that island's endemic species (later joined by those of Santa Fe and Rabida). Since an estimated 1,000 ships visited the archipelago during the 19th century – almost every one of which took between 60 and 90 tortoises – the total count is thought to approach 100,000.

As icing on the cake, whaling ships introduced black rats to the islands, a species that remains a major problem today. By the mid-1800s, though, the Galápagos had earned its reputation for *dry cruising,* because most of the whales in the vicinity had been hunted out. The discovery of petroleum in the late 19th century spelled the end of the whaling industry – not a moment too soon for the islands' inhabitants.

reach the Galápagos until regularly scheduled air service began in the early '70s.

Meanwhile, unrestricted immigration to the islands increased the discontent of island residents with their situation and the government on the mainland. Friction continues to this day, as settlers led by false preconceptions pour in and find much less than they expected. Water and electricity are scarce, and money is tight; the government is accused of concentrating on tourism at the expense of its own citizens. For its part, the government, in the uniform of the National Park Service, struggles to protect a fragile ecological balance from a 6 percent annual immigration rate and close to 171,000 visitors per year.

The archipelago was among the first 12 regions in the world to receive UNESCO protection in 1978. The 1986 Galápagos Marine Resources Reserve, which bestowed National

INTRODUCED SPECIES

By far the most serious threats to the ecosystems of the Galápagos are the descendants of the animals and plants left by settlers and visitors over the centuries. Only two of the major islands are free of exotic species, while the plants and animals on the rest of the islands are largely defenseless against 500 species of feral intruders. The most noxious intruders include 13 species of mammals and 10 species of birds. Hundreds of flora species pose a threat to native flora and fauna. Introductions still occur: The Norway rat arrived in 1983 and has spread to at least two islands already. Fruit flies recently arrived in San Cristóbal.

INTRODUCED ANIMALS

Most introduced species began as domestic animals that escaped into the wild. **Donkeys** can exist in lower, drier elevations, where they eat through cactus-tree trunks to get at the juicy pulp, killing the plant in the process. Scattered **horses** and **cattle** roam the highlands, and feral **pigs** gobble down turtle eggs, sometimes as quickly as the turtle lays them. Groups of **wild dogs** have reportedly staged inexplicable, bloodthirsty attacks on land iguana colonies. Hundreds of corpses have been left to rot on both Isabela and Santa Cruz.

   Cats revert to the wild almost instantly (just ask any cat owner) and are a major threat to bird chicks on many islands. **Rats** and **mice,** present since the first whaling ship came ashore, are among the most difficult species to control, as well as the most destructive. Almost every giant tortoise hatchling on Pinzon in the last century has fallen prey to

black rats, leaving an elderly population with little hope of reproducing. House mice began in settlers' homes and soon spread to many islands.

   Because their permeable skin makes it impossible for them to survive a long, dry ocean voyage, amphibians were the only one of five classes of vertebrates that hadn't colonized the Galápagos – that is, until 1998, when a small species of **tree frog** was first captured on Isabela and Santa Cruz. Scientists think the frogs arrived in cargo ships and were able to establish sustainable breeding populations during the particularly wet 1997-1998 El Niño season.

   Of all the introduced animals, **goats** have been the most serious threat. Thanks to their ability to eat almost anything (they can survive on seawater during droughts), goats can bulldoze their way across an island in no time. The tough animals eat plants down to the ground, leaving nothing for native animals to eat and causing severe erosion. Add to this mix the reproductive capabilities of a copying machine and you have a recipe for disaster; three goats left on Pinta in the late 1950s had generated more than 40,000 descendants by 1970. Today, only San Cristóbal and Santa Cruz have remnant goat populations.

INTRODUCED PLANTS

Not as obvious but just as deadly, introduced plants steal sun, water, and nutrients from native species. Introduced species have skyrocketed from 77 in 1971 – many brought by early settlers for food, medicine, and building ma-

Park status on the waters around the islands as well, was received particularly poorly, since it included a ban on unrestricted fishing in the local waters. Strikes and protest culminated in a group of machete-wielding sea-cucumber fishermen seizing the Darwin Center and threatening the life of tortoise Lonesome George. The Ecuadorian government backpedaled in response, opening the waters around the archipelago to limited commercial fisheries in 1995.

The most recent installment in the saga occurred in March 1998, when the Ecuadorian National Congress approved the long-awaited Special Law for the Galápagos. Aimed at conserving the islands' biodiversity while encouraging and regulating sustainable development, the law addresses the threat of introduced species through eradication and quarantine programs. It also restricts immigration and promotes local environmental education

terials – to almost 500 in 1997 (compared to only 560 native species). Today, vines such as the passionfruit and blackberry grow quickly into impenetrable thickets, and trees such as the guava and red quinine take over entire hillsides. It's estimated that the guava species *Psidium guajava* alone covers 50,000 hectares in the Galápagos.

SOLUTIONS

The Ministry of the Environment, the Ecuadorian National Park Service, and the Charles Darwin Research Center are joining efforts to rid the islands of introduced species. Each method has its drawbacks: hunting, the simplest solution, is difficult in the broken terrain; traps and poison may kill native species as well; and fencing is expensive and effective only with larger animals.

The SICGAL organization now checks all luggage and packages entering the islands or moving between islands for organic materials of any kind. This has discouraged many new importations and led to confiscations of animals, plants, and seeds. Families wishing to keep pets in their towns must register their neutered animals and produce health certificates; unregistered animals are destroyed.

The hard work is paying off. In 2002, a four-year campaign by the National Park Service and the Charles Darwin Research Center succeeded in ridding Santiago Island of 25,000 feral pigs. The 300,000 goats that infested Isabela have suffered a similar fate. After ground-pounding hunters reduced goat populations, a number of "Judas goats" were fitted with radio-tracking collars and brightly painted horns and released into the wild. When the naturally gregarious animals found a herd, they were located from the air, all the other animals shot and left to rot, and the process began again. As of 2003, some 125,000 goats had been killed this way, and the technique helped reduce Pinta's goat population from 30,000 to next to nothing. In 2006 goats were eradicated from Isabela and Pinta.

The disastrous El Niño of 1982–1983 actually helped an eradication campaign on Santiago by weakening goats and pigs. Park employees were able to kill 20,000 out of 100,000 goats and half of nearly 10,000 pigs. Black rats have been eliminated from Seymour North, fire ants eradicated from Marchena, and wild dog populations are being controlled.

Floreana's dark-rumped petrel is an encouraging success story. Formerly, large populations of petrels had been decimated by dogs, cats, rats, and pigs. (At one point, pigs ate so many petrels that farmers noticed their pork tasted faintly of fish from the contents of the seabirds' stomachs.) One study in the 1960s showed that only 4 out of 92 nests produced young. A predator-control program involving poisoned bait and traps has turned things around – today, four out of five petrels survive chickhood, instead of one out of five, as before.

Plans to re-introduce the endemic Floreana mockingbird to Floreana from Champion islet, where they are currently reproducing well, are also underway.

programs. The percentage of tourist revenue going to the park itself has been increased to 40 percent, and other badly needed funds are being redirected to the islands' inhabitants, earmarked for increased conservation efforts.

The law's most controversial section is proving to be the expansion of the Galápagos Marine Reserve from 15 to 40 nautical miles into the waters around the islands. Within these new boundaries—at 133,000 square kilometers, the country's second-largest marine reserve—only tourism and *"artesanal"* (i.e., local traditional) fishing are permitted.

Illegal fishing ships are still being caught and impounded, and some protests continue. In one instance, the Ecuadorian Marines had to be flown in. As a result, the Ecuadorian government has once again backed down, increasing lobster quotas and extending the fishing seasons. Emboldened fishermen are pushing for even more concessions.

On January 16, 2001, the captain of the Ecuadorian-registered tanker *Jessica* misjudged his entry into Shipwreck Bay on San Cristóbal Island. The ship ran aground and began leaking diesel fuel. Despite international cleanup efforts, approximately two-thirds of the ship's 240,000-gallon cargo, originally meant for tour boats, found its way into the pristine waters.

Fortunately, favorable winds and tides carried much of the fuel to the north and away from the islands. Small stretches of beach and some animals were contaminated, but on the whole, shoreline damage was kept to a minimum. The long-term effects of the spill on ocean-floor algae, the foundation of the islands' entire food chain, have yet to be determined, but the director of the National Park said he expected the ecosystem to recover fully within three–four years. The ship captain was sentenced to 90 days in jail. Currently, an insurance settlement of $3.375 million is under discussion.

The end of 2001 brought much better news: In December, UNESCO designated 133,000 square kilometers of marine reserve around the islands as a World Heritage Site. (It's also been labeled one of the Seven Underwater Wonders of the World by conservation groups.) Residents weren't universally thrilled, fearing it would hinder fishing and other sea-based businesses.

The oil spill did have one positive outcome: it spurred Ecuador to sign an accord with environmental groups to move toward clean, renewable energy systems in the islands. A wind-energy project has been installed on San Cristobal, providing around 60 percent of the island's power needs and replacing a diesel-powered plant; small boats are now required to replace polluting outboard motors with cleaner versions; and recycling systems are working in the towns.

The Natural World

Take five-and-twenty heaps of cinders dumped here and there in an outside city lot; imagine some of them magnified into mountains, and the vacant lot the sea; and you will have a fit idea of the general aspect of the Encantadas, or Enchanted Isles.

– Herman Melville, *Las Encantadas*, 1854

Life in the Galápagos is defined by geology, which here can be barren, beautiful, and busy in equal measure. The 13 volcanic islands of the province of Galápagos lie scattered over 60,000 square kilometers in the eastern Pacific Ocean. Actually the tips of underwater volcanoes, the islands become younger and higher to the west. Isabela, the largest island of the group (4,275 square kilometers), consists of six volcanic peaks joined by old lava flows. One of these, Cerro Azul, is the highest point in the archipelago at 1,689 meters. Sixteen tiny islets and almost 50 rocks complete the archipelago's 8,000 square kilometers of land. Land and sea meet in more than 1,350 kilometers of coastline. Most residents live on Santa Cruz Island, where Puerto Ayora is the largest city. Sleepy Puerto Baquerizo Moreno on San Cristóbal serves as the provincial capital, and Puerto Villamil on Isabela is the islands' third largest town.

VOLCANIC ORIGINS

The Galápagos sit directly over a hotspot in the Pacific crust plate, where underlying magma bulges much closer to the surface than usual. Millions of years ago, molten rock began to bubble up through the crust, cooling in the seawater and piling into mountains that eventually poked above the surface.

As the Pacific crust plate slowly grinds its way southeast under the Nazca plate, which supports the South American mainland, the volcanoes were carried along as well. New volcanoes quickly formed to take the place of older ones and were slowly worn away by the sea and weather, resulting in a rough chain of islands trailing off toward the mainland. (The Hawaiian Islands are also hotspot volcanoes.)

All of this slow bubbling and sliding produced a few interesting side effects. The islands that currently make up the archipelago are about 3.5 million years old—geologic newborns—but the entire process has been going on for much longer. This means that many more volcanoes have come and gone, weathered away to nothing beneath the seas to the east, than remain visible today (a crucial clue in an evolutionary puzzle concerning the iguana). The islands will eventually disappear, as the Nazca plate drives them under the continent faster than the hotspot can push out new ones. Don't worry, though—we're only talking a few centimeters per year, and the whole process will take about 50 million years.

VOLCANIC ACTIVITY

Clues to the Galápagos's volcanic origins are everywhere, and new scars form daily. Beaches

pahoehoe lava

© JULIAN SMITH

of volcanic minerals and jagged spires of tuff (compacted volcanic ash and debris) dot the coast, whereas farther up in the highlands, you can visit collapsed calderas and lava tunnels, which formed when lava continued flowing within a hardened outer layer.

On more recent flows, such as the one in Sullivan Bay, it's possible to distinguish the two main types of basaltic lava found in the islands. Ropy pahoehoe (pa-HOY-hoy) lava, from the Polynesian word for "calm sea," is formed when a cooled surface layer wrinkles over a liquid base like the skin on cooling hot chocolate. Jagged a'a (AH-ah) lava contains more silicates and starts out stickier, cooling quickly and completely into a super-stucco surface that's tricky to negotiate on foot. The name comes from the Polynesian word for "choppy sea," but it's more easily remembered as the sound you'd make walking over it in bare feet.

The islands of Marchena, Pinta, Isabela, and Fernandina, farthest north and west, are the youngest and most geologically active. Isabela

© JULIAN SMITH

lava gulls

AN IGUANA MYSTERY SOLVED

Scientist Vincent Sarich raised an interesting question in his 1983 scientific paper, "Are the Galápagos Iguanas Older Than the Galápagos?" While the current estimate for the age of the archipelago is between two and three million years, naturalists were sure that marine and land iguanas must have needed at least 15 million years to diverge so completely from their common mainland ancestor. In short, the islands weren't nearly old enough to have given endemic species sufficient time to evolve into their present state.

Careful analysis of the ocean floor to the east yielded an answer. Six hundred kilometers from the mainland to the east of the archipelago, the remains of old, sunken islands were found, formerly part of the Galápagos group. Before plate drift had carried them east and erosion had reduced them to undersea nubs, these islands may have been around for as long as the Galápagos hot spot has been active (more than 80 million years). Present species would then have had ample time to arrive, evolve, and move to the present islands.

and Fernandina blew off steam, and occasionally much more, well into the 20th century. In 1954, a passing film crew noticed a strange new white beach in Urbina Bay on the west coast of Isabela. On closer investigation, they found that an entire stretch of shoreline—coral, fish, and all—had just been raised six meters above sea level by volcanic pressure underneath. Fernandina's latest eruption in 1995 lasted three months and sent a 100-meter-wide flow of lava five kilometers into the sea.

THE SEA

The islands are pushed and pulled by several ocean currents, which are stirred by trade winds dragging over the water's surface and intensified by the earth's rotation. The Peru (or Humboldt) Current, one of the world's grandest, sweeps north along the coast of Chile and Peru, bringing cold waters into the Equatorial region. Subdivided into coastal and oceanic currents, the Peru Current parts from the coast near the equator to flow west and wash the Galápagos with its cool waters. The Panama Current flows down from Central America, turning west toward the archipelago near the coast of mainland Ecuador.

West of the islands, the warm Equatorial Current (split into northern and southern

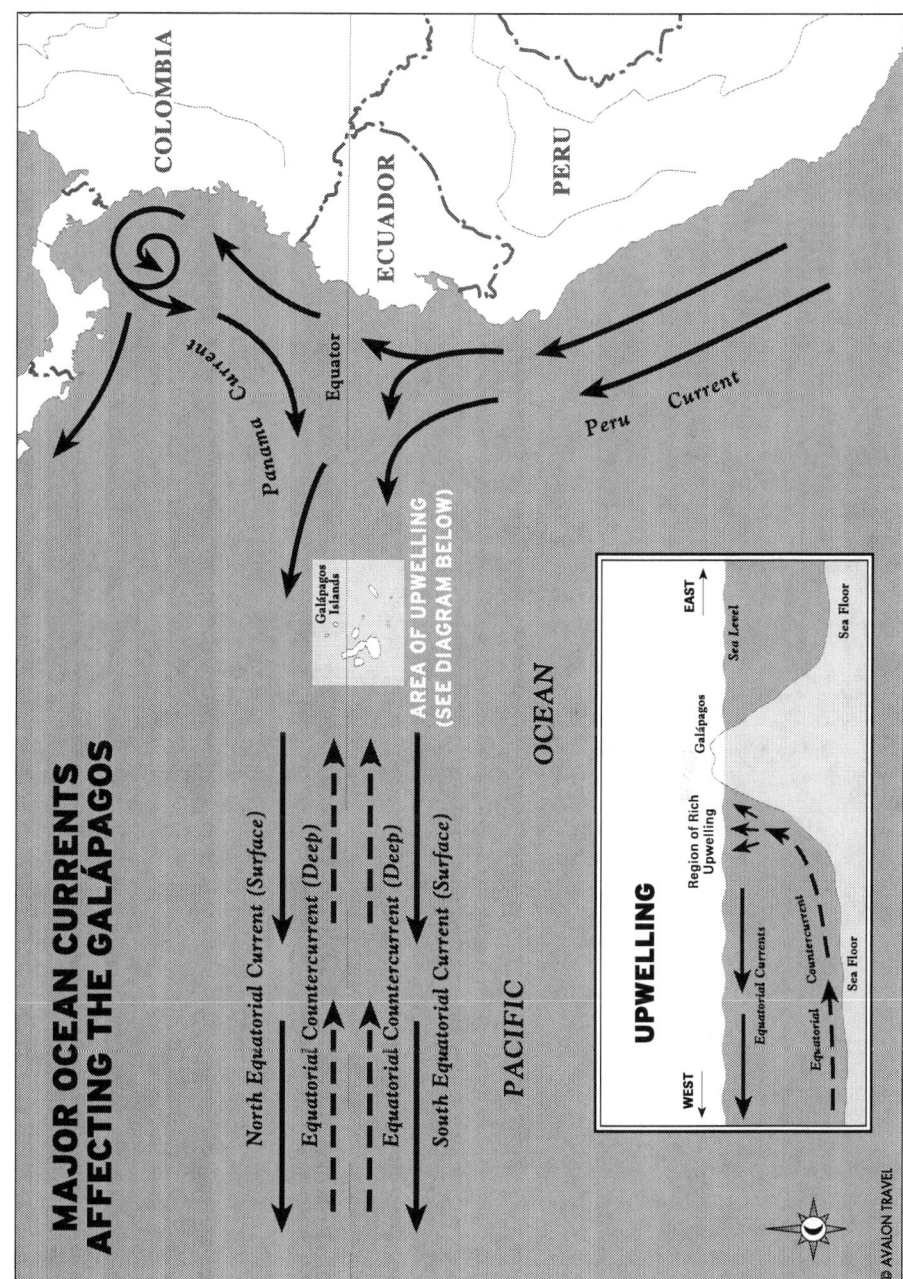

MAJOR OCEAN CURRENTS
AFFECTING THE GALÁPAGOS

COLOMBIA

ECUADOR

PERU

Panama Current

Equator

Peru Current

Galápagos
Islands

AREA OF UPWELLING
(SEE DIAGRAM BELOW)

PACIFIC   OCEAN

North Equatorial Current (Surface)

Equatorial Countercurrent (Deep)

Equatorial Countercurrent (Deep)

South Equatorial Current (Surface)

UPWELLING

WEST

EAST

Sea Level

Sea Floor

Galápagos

Region of Rich
Upwelling

Equatorial Currents

Equatorial Countercurrent

Sea Floor

© AVALON TRAVEL

sections) continues the surface thrust of the Peru Current west into the Pacific. Deep beneath the water's surface, meanwhile, the Equatorial Counter Current—also called the Cromwell Current—rushes toward the Galápagos from the west. Upon encountering the westernmost islands in the archipelago, the countercurrent is deflected upward, bringing with it cool, nutrient-rich water from the depths of the Pacific.

The countercurrent isn't as constant as the other currents—it flows more during the dry season—but it's possibly the most important one of all. The western upwelling, 5–10°C cooler than the surface waters, is crucial to the marine habitat of the islands. Algae thrive on the nutrients, attracting fish and marine invertebrates that are more suited to the coastal waters than the middle of the Pacific. Larger marine mammals such as whales and dolphins follow these fish, and terrestrial animals and birds depend on the bounty of the surrounding sea. Galápagos penguins and flightless cormorants wait for the countercurrent to begin their breeding season.

CLIMATE
The archipelago's subtropical climate is almost completely determined by sea currents, whose varying temperatures bring seasons that differ only in cloud cover and the amount and type of precipitation. Smack on the equator, the islands enjoy 12 hours of sunlight per day throughout the year.

Seasons
The hot or **rainy season,** late November–June, arrives when the Panama Current warms the nearby waters to 26°C. Daily showers bring 6–10 centimeters of precipitation per month. Although there is less chance of a completely dry day during the hot season, you'll encounter more warm, sunny days per month than you will in the cool season. Average temperatures climb into the 30s, with February and March the warmest and sunniest months.

The June–November **dry season** arrives with the colder (20°C) waters from the Peru Current. Average temperatures drop to less than 27°C, and any precipitation that falls is usually in the form of *garúa*, a misty drizzle that gathers in the highlands. This lingering fog forms at the inversion layer—the intersection between lower ocean-cooled air and warmer air above it—at around 400–600 meters. There are fewer chances of outright rain, but overcast days are common. Lower elevations remain dry and dead-looking, especially from August to November.

Altitudinal Variations
The climate at sea level can be hot and arid. Rain is scarce, with minor drizzles and mist during the cool season. Average temperatures drop into the teens as you climb to 500 meters, where the climate begins to resemble subtropical and temperate zones. The highlands on the larger islands (Fernandina, Isabela, Santa Cruz, and San Cristóbal) bear a distinctive type of cloud forest, complete with mist, mosses, lichens, grass, and trees. Temperatures up here, amplified by the dampness, can get downright chilly.

El Niño
There was a time toward the end of the 20th century when it seemed as if everything from heat spells to failed marriages was being blamed on this mysterious climatic phenomenon. Named for the Christ child because of its tendency to appear near the Christmas holidays, El Niño (and its climatic cousin, La Niña) arrives periodically to create havoc throughout the Pacific basin.

When El Niño is in town, December–March in certain years, warm waters from the north surge suddenly and force the Peru Current south for anywhere from 6 to 18 months. Ocean temperatures rise, clouds gather, and 6–10 centimeters more rain falls per month than average. The extra moisture is welcomed by the thirsty islands, but occasionally El Niño brings too much of a good thing. Extreme El Niño seasons in 1982–1983 and 1997–1998 wrought havoc on the archipelago's fragile ecosystem, causing high mortality among marine

THE INCREDIBLE SHRINKING IGUANAS

Although the 1997-1998 El Niño didn't hit the Galápagos as hard as it did mainland Ecuador, it still had a large effect on the island's inhabitants. One of the most curious results was reported in the journal *Nature* by Martin Wikelski, professor of ecology, ethology, and evolution at the University of Illinois at Urbana-Champaign.

In examining data collected since 1987, Wikelski and his coworkers noticed that marine iguanas shrank when the marine algae they feed on died during the El Niño season, then regrew to their original size when food became plentiful again. The study was the first conclusive finding of a shrinking adult mammal, and it countered an unofficial dogma among scientists that animals, well, just don't do that.

On one island, Wikelski found that some iguanas lost not only half their body weight but also a quarter of their length during the 1997-1998 El Niño season. They're not sure how exactly the iguanas managed it, but the scientists hypothesized that the animals may have somehow absorbed part of their skeletons. By becoming smaller, an iguana would increase its chances of survival by making it easier to forage and be warmed by the sun. When food became plentiful again, the iguanas started growing back to their original size to increase their odds of winning territories and reproducing. "You want to be the largest one during the non-El Niño years," summed up the report, "and then you want to be the smallest one during the El Niño years."

The ability to control the loss and recovery of bone mass may eventually have significant implications in human health care. The U.S. national expenditure for osteoporosis – a medical condition in which bones become brittle and break easily, especially in the elderly – was estimated at $10 billion in 1987, and astronauts are known to lose bone density during extended periods in space.

iguanas, sea lions, waved albatrosses, penguins, and boobies.

FLORA AND FAUNA

Life in the Galápagos is a study in extremes. These parched, rocky islands spread under the equatorial sun are surprisingly rich in life. The only way to survive here, it seems, is to adapt, which means a high level of **endemic species**—those found nowhere else on earth. The Galápagos has 1,900 endemic species out of 5,000 total: 32 percent of the plants, almost half of all birds, half of all shore fish and insects, and 90 percent of the reptiles have become so specifically adapted to life in the islands that they hardly resemble their original mainland ancestors at all.

In contrast, the fragility of the Galápagos ecosystem shows itself in a low level of **diversity:** There aren't as many different species as one would expect. This paucity of species has created a delicate balance—certain species, both plant and animal, are completely dependent on others.

Colonization

By now, you've probably asked yourself the most obvious question about the islands' inhabitants: How did they get there? The Galápagos were never connected to the mainland, and 1,000 kilometers of open water is a long swim. As impressive as it seems, though, most species arrived more or less under their own power. Fish and marine mammals cruising the currents might have bumped into the islands and decided to stay, whereas land birds blown off course wouldn't have known the way back to the mainland even if they had wanted to leave. Seabirds and migrant species, knowing a good fishing spot when they saw one, might have returned to breed year after year. Insects and plant seeds could also have been carried from the South American continent by high winds, whereas other seeds were probably excreted by birds or arrived stuck to their feet.

As for terrestrial reptiles and rats, the generally accepted explanation involves the large rafts of vegetation that still wash down

Ecuador's ocean-bound rivers. Any animals or plants that happened to be aboard, provided they could survive the journey, stood a slim chance of riding the currents all the way to the Galápagos. (Some rafts are even large enough to support living trees—another colonization possibility.) With their ability to slow their own metabolism, reptiles are particularly suited for such a long, difficult journey. On the other hand, large mammals would tend to die of dehydration, and amphibians would dry up during the trip, which explains why there weren't any of either group on the islands before the arrival of humans.

Marinelife

The Galápagos are every bit as spectacular beneath the water's surface as above it. A staggering diversity of life inhabits a wide range of marine habitats, from mangrove estuaries to lava-rocky tide pools, volcanic beaches to the sandy bottom. About 50 marine species are endemic, in a percentage comparable to endemic numbers on land. All of this is a result of a few climatic factors—a combination of warm and cold currents and the El Niño phenomenon, which warms things drastically every so often—that have turned the Galápagos into a natural marine reserve in the middle of the Pacific.

Because the ravages of hunting have not, for the most part, reached far below the surface, the same animal fearlessness is found beneath the waves as on land. Sea turtles sleeping near the surface will only steer casually away upon being awakened. Sea lions almost treat you like one of the pack—just stay out of the way of the territorial bulls. And in the deep, it's almost as if you weren't there at all, as huge schools of fish engulf divers in living clouds of silver.

Taxonomy

A brief explanation of taxonomy (the scientific classification of living things) should help neophytes better appreciate the natural history of the islands. Every single organism ever discovered has been given a unique spot in the hierarchy of taxonomic divisions, pinpointed by a lengthy label of Latin and Greek terms. The term you'll hear over and over again in talk of the Galápagos ecology is **species,** the fundamental taxonomic unit that's loosely defined as a group of organisms sharing many common characteristics (abbreviated "sp" or "spp"). Species usually live in a specific area and are only able to successfully reproduce with each other. The next two categories above species are genus and family.

Plants and animals are most often referred to by their **common name,** as well as their **scientific name,** usually written as the genus and species. Animals in the Galápagos also have Spanish names, of course, only some of which are related to their common (English) names. For example, the blue-footed booby (common name) is called the *piquero patas azules* in Spanish (blue-footed lancer) and saddled with the scientific name *Sula nebuoxi* (genus Sula, species nebouxii).

REPTILES

The reptiles of the Galápagos define the islands more than any other group of animals. Here, reptiles still rule the earth, giving a taste of what the rest of the planet may have been like tens of millions of years ago. More than 90 percent of the reptile species in the Galápagos are endemic, a testament to their ability to enter a state of hibernation-like torpor that would have allowed their ancestors to survive the long ocean crossing. In addition to the reptiles described below, the Galápagos harbors five endemic species of **gecko** and three species of **Galápagos snake.**

Giant Tortoise

These creaking giants, with skin like the world's oldest leather jacket, are the largest in the world. They're found only here and on a few islands in the Indian Ocean, notably in the Seychelles off the coast of Tanzania. The Galápagos species, *Geochelone elephantopus,* can reach 250 kilograms and nobody knows how what age. Dependable records top out at 100 years, but some stories have turtles lasting more than 200 years. During your visit to the Darwin Center in Puerto Ayora, notice the smooth domes of the tortoises in captivity, and think how long it must have taken to wear those huge shells down.

The shell of a giant tortoise reveals which island, or at least what type of island, its owner hails from. Saddle-shaped shells, high in front and the back, evolved on low, arid islands where tortoises must lift their heads as high as possible to browse tall vegetation. (The tortoises' necks and legs are also longer on these islands.) Semicircular domed shells come from higher, lusher islands with vegetation that grows low to the ground. Males have larger and longer tails, with a concave plastron (bottom plate) that helps them mount females during mating.

During mating season, the only time tortoises make any noise, unearthly groans echo for kilometers as males joust for dominance— a relatively simple showdown in which the higher head wins. When her eggs are ready to hatch, the female softens the soil with urine before digging a nest for as long as five hours. A single layer of tennis-ball-sized eggs is covered with six inches of packed earth that soon dries hard. The nest is a surprisingly delicate system: The top layer of mud must keep the heat and moisture levels within a narrow range, because a temperature difference of a few degrees Celsius decides whether the offspring will be male, female, or stillborn. Broods hatch during the first months of the year.

Tortoises spend much of their lives in a state of torpor, when their metabolism and body temperature slow significantly. This ability allows them to survive dry periods on the island with a minimum of food and water. But when the rains do come, look out—on Alcedo Volcano on Isabela, the wet season is greeted by a slow-motion orgy of eating, drinking, mating, and wallowing in new pools of water. By nighttime, everyone ends up in the mud, snoozing contentedly in large groups.

When the islands were first discovered, there were as many as 250,000 tortoises, and 14 islands each had their own species. Today, there are only about 15,000 left, and three of those species (Santa Fe, Floreana, and Fernandina) are extinct. The Pinta species is represented by one surviving member named Lonesome George. Whalers were once the tortoises' main enemy, but today the danger comes from introduced animal species. Pigs can dig up dozens of nests in no time, hatchlings fall prey to cats and rats, and larger tortoises can be killed by dogs. Even if they do survive to adulthood, tortoises often have to compete with burros, goats, and cattle for food.

Marine Iguanas

The only true marine lizard in the world, *Amblyrhynchus cristatus* evolved from a terrestrial species that took to the water to survive. In a short time, evolutionarily speaking (only two–three million years), marine iguanas have adapted well to feed on coastal seaweed. A flattened snout allows closer munching, a vertically flattened tail propels better in the water, long claws grab underwater rocks firmly, and a pair of salt-eliminating glands in the nostrils cleanse sea salt from their system. As a result, they're prodigious divers that are able to stay under for well more than an hour by lowering their heart rate by half.

Anywhere from 200,000 to 300,000 marine iguanas inhabit the Galápagos. Males can reach a little more than one meter in length and weigh up to 20 kilograms, with the average size increasing toward the western islands. Bright colorings attract females during the dry season; Espanola's iguanas are particularly colorful. Despite their prehistoric appearance (one was used as a model for the updated version of *Godzilla*), the iguanas are harmless.

Marine iguanas feed on shallow-growing seaweed, shunning the tough, brown stuff for tender green and red morsels. This inconspicuous but surprisingly nutritious plant grows like, well, a weed—a one-kilometer patch can quintuple its mass in less than two weeks and support up to 3,000 iguanas at once. Marine iguanas feed for about an hour every day, always at low tide. Basking in the sun helps each iguana generate enough heat to digest a bellyful of cellulose.

Regulating body heat is a prime concern, especially after a long dive. Like all reptiles, marine iguanas are ectotherms, meaning their internal body temperatures are at the mercy of outside temperatures. Males prefer to dive during the hottest part of the day to keep cool. On shore, the trick becomes not warming back up too much: Lava-rock temperatures can climb more than 40°C, and iguanas die if their body temperature rises above 45°C. To remedy this problem, iguanas face the sun, exposing as little surface area as possible, and raise their bodies off the ground to allow air to circulate underneath. On cold days and at night, iguanas congregate into huge piles to conserve heat.

Marine iguana populations fell slightly over the years as a result of hunting by early visitors, but recent El Niño seasons in the 1980s and 1990s struck much more deeply. Abnormally warm waters killed the shallow-growing algae, spelling doom for those animals not strong enough to dive to reach deeper algae. Since then, in a handy example of evolution in action, marine iguanas have become slightly larger, and females breed every year instead of every two as before.

Land Iguanas

The seven subspecies of land iguana (*Conolophus* spp.) in the Galápagos have evolved a pale yellow coloring, in contrast to their mainland ancestors' arboreal green. Land iguanas evolved from a similar species as their seagoing relatives—the difference being that by the time land iguanas' ancestors arrived at the islands, enough ground vegetation had grown that they didn't have to take to the water to survive.

Land iguanas live in dry areas, where they spend the night in dugout burrows to conserve heat. Their menu is mostly vegetarian: any plant within reach gets chomped, including berries, flowers, fruits, and cactus pads, spines and all. Land iguanas get much of their water from food. After digging their way out of the nest, tiny newborn iguanas must avoid hawks, owls, and introduced predators until they're large enough to defend themselves. Males can reach 13 kilograms and live more

CHARLES, LEAVE THE IGUANAS ALONE

The father of evolutionary theory would have been booted from the Royal Society for the Prevention of Cruelty to Animals because of his own accounts of tormenting, eating, and expressing general negativity toward the Galápagos's inhabitants during his visit. In the *Voyage of the Beagle,* he wrote of dining on giant tortoises: "The breast-plate roasted . . . with the flesh on it, is very good; and the young tortoises make excellent soup; but otherwise the meat to my taste is indifferent."

He went on to describe the marine iguana as "a hideous-looking creature, of a dirty black colour, stupid, and sluggish in its movements." One hapless iguana Darwin repeatedly threw into the ocean kept returning to the same place on shore. This "singular piece of apparent stupidity" caused the naturalist to wonder about the animal's response to predators: "Urged by a fixed and hereditary instinct that the shore is its place of safety, whatever emergency there may be, it there takes refuge" – meddling naturalist or not.

Land iguanas fared little better. "Like their brothers the sea-kind," he noted, "they are ugly animals, of a yellowish orange beneath, and of a brownish red colour above: From their low facial angle they have a singularly stupid appearance." Even in the dinner pot, the land iguana just couldn't measure up: "These lizards, when cooked, yield a white meat, which is liked by those whose stomachs soar above all prejudices." After watching one land iguana dig a nest hole "for a long time," Darwin proceeded to yank it back out by the tail.

"At this it was greatly astonished," he wrote, "and stared me in the face, as much as to say, 'What made you pull my tail?'"

than 60 years. Maturity comes between ages 10 and 15, when adult males begin a career of vigorously defending a specific territory, with head-nodding threats that often end in battle.

As a result of hunting and introduced species, the land iguana species on Santiago and Baltra have become extinct, and those on other islands are in trouble. A captive-breeding program at the Darwin Center attempts to maintain threatened populations at viable levels. Only Fernandina's iguanas have avoided outside intrusion, and they're among the largest in the islands.

Sea Turtles

The eastern **Pacific green turtle** *(Chelonia mydas agassisi)* is the most common species in the islands. Called *tortugas negras* (black turtles) in Spanish, Pacific greens depend on the Galápagos for nesting beaches. Beyond that, it's not known whether they live here year-round or migrate periodically to the mainland. Green sea turtles average around 100 kilograms and can often be spotted sleeping on shallow sandy bottoms or mating in open water. Awkward at or above the surface, sea turtles glide gorgeously beneath, where they can hold their breath for hours. They're often seen coming up for air alongside anchored boats.

Also present in the islands, although rarely seen, are the **Pacific leatherback** *(Dermochelys coriacea)* and the **Indo-Pacific hawksbill** *(Eretmochely imbricata).*

Lava Lizard

Seven species of the ubiquitous lava lizard *(Tropidurus albemarlensis)* scurry over sand and rock on almost every island. Larger males can reach 30 centimeters, and females can be identified by red throat patches. Lava lizards feed democratically, gulping down insects, plants, and even each other. In turn, they're pursued by many larger birds, who are only occasionally fooled by the lizards' break-away tails.

Like soldiers at boot camp, male lava lizards do pushups constantly, to the point that their Spanish name *(lagartija)* has become a slang term for pushup. The pattern of ups and downs is different for different island species and is thought to defend territory, as well as regulate body temperature.

MAMMALS

Only six species of mammals originally called the Galápagos home, and four of those arrived by swimming or flying. The long ocean crossing (at least two weeks by floating raft) is too long for most mammals to survive; in fact, Galápagos rice rats set a world record for long-distance colonization.

Galápagos Sea Lion

Somehow feline and canine at the same time, the Galápagos sea lion *(Zalophus californianus wollebacki)* is a smaller cousin of the California sea lion. (Males in the Galápagos reach only 250 kilograms in size.) Their charming snouts, whiskers, and dark eyes belie a voice that sounds like the winner of a belching contest—even a newborn pup can bleat like a Billy goat coughing up a hairball.

© JULIAN SMITH

Galápagos sea lions

Some 50,000 sea lions sprawl over beaches and rocks throughout the islands—prolonged snoozing helps replenish oxygen used up during long, deep dives after fish. Sharks and killer whales are the sea lion's chief predators. Sea-lion bulls defend beach harems—short stretches of sand filled with females and pups—by patrolling loudly just offshore. Any male who is careless enough to approach the boundary is confronted immediately; the winner is usually the one who can raise his snout higher. Although most of this posturing is harmless, sea lion attacks are the most common cause of animal injury in the Galápagos. Steer well clear of patrolling males, especially when snorkeling.

Galápagos Fur Seal

With its small external ears and strong propulsive forward flippers, the Galápagos fur seal (*Arctocephalus galapagoensis*) isn't really a true seal (family Phocidae) at all. Like the larger Galápagos sea lion, the fur seal is a member of the eared-seal family Otariidae. Fur seals are smaller than sea lions, with a thick, furry coat that traces their ancestry to the cold coasts of Peru and Chile.

This luxurious coat almost led to the fur seal's extinction in the 19th century. The warm, two-layered pelt was in high demand in Europe and the United States, leading to unchecked slaughter at the hands of hunters. One ship in 1823 reported a take of 5,000 skins in two months. By the turn of the 20th century, the seal was thought to be extinct—a California Academy of Sciences expedition in 1905 found only one seal in an entire year.

Fortunately, the fur seal has made a comeback, despite a low birth rate of one pup every two years. Today, 30,000–40,000 fur seals inhabit the northern and western islands of Pinta, Marchena, Santiago, Isabela, and Fernandina.

Whales and Dolphins

Several cetaceans (completely aquatic mammals) can be seen around the islands. Those without teeth use hairy plates of baleen in their jaws to strain gallons of tiny creatures from the water. The **blue whale,** the largest animal in the world, is an occasional visitor to the archipelago, and the more common **humpback whale** *(Megaptera novaeangliae)* can reach 16 meters. The sight of one of these giants breaching completely out of the water—most often seen west of Isabela and Fernandina—is awe-inspiring. Smaller baleen species include finback, Sei, Bryde's, and Minke whales.

Toothed cetaceans eat larger prey, including fish and squid. Black-and-white **killer whales** *(Orcinus orca)* are the true lions of the sea. The sight of a tall, black dorsal fin is enough to clear a beach of sea lions in an instant. A population of **sperm whales** *(Physete macrocephalus)* is slowly recovering from the depredations of 19th-century whalers. Three resident species of **dolphin** surf the bow waves of cruising ships with unmistakable glee. Schools of up to 100 can be seen leaping in unison through the waves.

Bats and Rats

Two endemic species of bats made the long crossing—probably by accident—to make their home in the Galápagos. Two species of rice rats are left from an original seven. The rest were driven to extinction by the Norwegian black rat *(Rattus rattus),* which was introduced by visiting ships and is now a major threat to native species.

SEABIRDS

With nothing but water in every direction, the Galápagos are a perfect stopover for wide-ranging seabirds. Estimates range as high as 750,000 in the islands at any one time. Because they can come and go freely, seabirds have evolved fewer endemic species in the Galápagos compared to other types of birds. Out of the 19 species of seabirds on the islands, only five are endemic: the Galápagos penguin, flightless cormorant, waved albatross, lava gull, and swallow-tailed gull. Of these, only the last three can fly.

Boobies

Named after the Spanish word *bobo* (clown), boobies are the awkward but endearing mascots of the Galápagos. They belong to the same family as gannets (Sulidae), whom they resemble, with their large webbed feet, round heads, and long pointed beaks. All boobies catch fish with astounding plunges into the water from midair. You'll see blue-footed boobies doing this most often near the shore—a crash into the water inches from the base of rocky cliffs, a second of silence, then a pop to the surface, and *gulp*—down goes a fish. Air sacs in their skulls diffuse the shock of impact, and closed-beak nostrils keep salt water out. Boobies typically lay two or three eggs to ensure that at least one (and often only one) chick survives to adolescence. This brutally effective evolutionary insurance policy often involves larger chicks killing their smaller siblings.

Blue-footed boobies *(Sula nebouxii)* symbolize the Galápagos in the minds of much of the world, helped by countless T-shirts, hats, postcards, and posters. About 30 percent of the world's population nests in the islands—close to 10,000 pairs—where they feed close to shore. Males and females both have the famous neon-blue feet, so the only way to tell the sexes apart is by the size of their pupils (smaller in males) and the sound of their calls (females honk, males whistle). Males show off their feet during the courtship dance, a high-stepping ritual designed to show off sexual maturity and good genes—the bluer, the better. This strange ceremony is both comic and thought-provoking. As Kurt Vonnegut writes in his novel *Galapagos*, it "seems to have absolutely no connection with the elements of booby survival, with nesting or fish. What does it have to do with, then? Dare we call it 'religion?' Or, if we lack that sort of courage, might we at least call it 'art?'"

Blue-foots nest on the ground, where they scrape a shallow depression that becomes surrounded by a white ring of guano. Lacking the usual avian incubating pouch, parents keep the eggs warm on top of their feet, which are richly veined with warm blood vessels. After hatching, any chick that ends up outside the nest ring is as good as dead, ignored by its parents and pecked at by its siblings if it tries to reenter.

© JULIAN SMITH

blue-footed boobies

There are more **red-footed boobies** *(Sula sula)* than any other booby species in the Galápagos (a quarter of a million pairs), but they're also the least often seen. Although the world's largest colony of red-foots nests on Tower Island, its inhabitants are usually feeding far out to sea. Red-footed boobies are the smallest on the islands and have blue bills and brown plumage (a few have white feathers). Their relatively small feet, tipped with small claws, allow them to nest in trees.

The beautiful **masked boobies** *(Sula dactylatra)* nest on cliff edges because, as the largest booby species, they have a harder time taking off from level ground. Most of the masked boobies in the world nest in the Galápagos, giving you a good opportunity to see their stunning plumage: one of the purest whites in the animal kingdom, with a black eye mask and black wing edges.

Waved Albatross

Nearly the entire world population of the waved albatross *(Diomedea irrorata)*—some 12,000 pairs—nest on Española Island. Bulging white eyebrows atop cream-colored feathers give albatrosses a refined yet slightly comical appearance (think Groucho Marx in a nice suit). As graceful as it is soaring on its two-meter wings, the waved albatross is a duck out of water on land, waddling around like a sailor after too long at sea. The air-to-land transition seems to be a bit of a problem, too, as landings often end in a flailing tumble of feathers and squawks. Granted, many albatrosses have been cruising the thermals of the South Pacific for as long as three–four years without landing. The most successful albatross launch is a seaward leap off a cliff into a headwind.

For a long time, waved albatross couples were thought to mate for life, which can mean a 50-year commitment. The pair bond is reinforced through an elaborate courtship display, an ecstatic ritual that peaks in October and is worth scheduling a visit around. Bills clatter, circle, and point at the sky as participants perform an exaggerated version of their normal swaying walk.

Recent research, however, has cast some doubts on this astounding display of fidelity. One study recorded 1,724 matings among some 300 albatrosses over 40 days—one female mated 85 times with 49 different males—and found through DNA testing that one out of every four chicks was not actually sired by the bird that acted as its "father." Practices such as adoption, adultery, and even rape have been observed among the graceful seabirds.

After going on long hunting junkets, parents stuff chicks to bursting with up to two liters of a predigested mixture of fish and squid. Researcher Bryan Nelson described the result: "For the first four months of its life the chick is hardly more than a great, oil-filled skin, covered in matted brown down. It is grotesque with the fascination of the truly ugly."

Galápagos Penguin

Short-listed for the Cutest Endemic Species award, the Galápagos penguin *(Sheniscus mendiculus)* seems as out of place in the hot, dry islands as a polar bear at a beach party. At 35 centimeters high, it's one of the smallest penguin species. Having evolved from the Humboldt penguins that inhabit the Patagonian coasts of Peru and Chile, the Galápagos penguin is the only penguin found north of the equator. Because they still retain much of their original insulation, Galápagos penguins have to struggle to stay cool in the hot sun. The classic wings-out pose lowers a bird's temperature, but it occasionally comes down to a choice between the cooking of the nest eggs (which must be continually shaded by day) or the parents (who are forced to jump into the water). With only 3,000–5,000 breeding pairs, Galápagos penguins are one of the rarest species of seabirds in the world.

Frigatebirds

The bad boys of the Galápagos are notorious for making a living stealing food from other species. This type of feeding, called kleptoparasitism, is the reason frigatebirds were named after fast colonial-era warships. A forked tail, backswept wings, and extremely low weight for their size make them faster and more maneuverable then anything else in the air. They can often be seen harassing a booby returning with fish for a chick until the parent disgorges its meal; the frigatebird will then scoop its pilfered food out of the air. They're not above stealing food right out of a chick's mouth on the ground, either. This light-fingered lifestyle has evolved partly because these birds can't dive for their own food—with only vestigial preening glands, a frigatebird can't waterproof its feathers, and it sinks like a stone if it becomes waterlogged.

The males' distinctive red throat pouch is inflated to attract females. Once they go to the bother of pumping it up with air, they'll leave it inflated all day. A female drifting over a group of males during the mating season elicits waves of pouch-waving, bill-rattling, and calling meant to attract her to particular nests. Pairs mate for life, and chicks take up to one year to learn the thieving acrobatics of survival.

The male **magnificent frigatebird** *(Fregata magnificens)* has a purple-tinged nape and a white patch on the breast conveniently shaped like an M. An all-white breast and greenish neck and chest distinguish the male **great frigatebird** *(Fregata minor)*.

Flightless Cormorant

You'll have to make it out to Fernandina and western Isabela to see some of the 2,000 pairs of flightless cormorants *(Nannopterum harrisi)*, one of the few bird species in the world that has lost the ability to fly. The aquatic birds are a study of evolution in action from their steel blue eyes to their asymmetrical feet. Millennia of diving after fish, eels, and octopi on the near-shore bottom, combined with a lack of predators on land, have allowed the cormorants' wings and tail to atrophy to vestigial nubs. The typical avian keeled breastbone— a solid anchor for strong flying muscles—has vanished in flightless cormorants, whereas their long snakelike necks, strong kicking legs, and huge webbed feet make them experts at pursuing fish underwater. Flightless cormorants still haven't forgotten their roots, though, and they

stand patiently to dry their ragged wings every time they emerge from the water.

Cormorant nests are an impressive conglomeration of flotsam and twigs that are in use year-round by breeding pairs. The nests are often set precariously close to the waterline, and many eggs are washed away by high spring tides.

Endemic Gulls

Close to 15,000 pairs of **swallow-tailed gulls** *(Creagrus furcatus)* nest throughout the islands. They're one of the prettier gulls around, with a charcoal-colored head and white and gray body highlighted by red feet and a distinctive red eye ring. Unlike most other gulls, swallow-tails feed out to sea at night, pointing boat captains the way toward land in the morning. The **lava gull** *(Larus fuliginosus)* is thought to be the rarest gull in the world, consisting of only about 400 mating pairs nesting in the Galápagos. Their dark gray plumage blends into the lava rocks they prefer, but their obnoxious chortle gives them away immediately.

Other Species

A distinctive chattering call signals the return of the **red-billed tropicbird** *(Phaethon aethereus)* from feeding far out to sea. If they make it past the frigatebirds, their next task is to pull off a swooping landing into the windy cliffside nests they prefer. Tropicbirds have a fragile beauty, with a gray and white body and long, flowing white pintails capped by a red bill and a black mask.

If you've spent any time near the coast, you'll undoubtedly recognize the **brown pelican** *(Pelecanus occidentalis)*, groups of which are often seen at sunset skimming regally in formation, inches above the water. It's one of the largest and most commonly seen Galápagos seabirds, but actually one of the smaller species of pelican. It may not seem designed for it, but this ungainly-looking seabird plunges into the ocean over and over to capture food. After filling its 14-liter beak pouch with water on impact, the pelican filters out the fish and gulps them down.

The western cliffs of Isabela are home to the **brown noddy** *(Anous stolidus)*, a tern-like bird that nests in caves and dark niches. Noddies bring a classic beauty to the Galápagos, with an avian tuxedo of smart gray plumage punctuated by a white forehead and eye patches. You'll occasionally see them waiting on pelicans' heads for scraps.

If you happen to see a small black bird skimming the water for fish, it could be one of a few species. Both the **Audubon's shearwater** *(Puffinus l'herminieri)* and the larger **dark-rumped petrel** *(Pterodroma pharopygia)* have black backs and white fronts. The latter, also called the Hawaiian petrel, is nocturnal and highly endangered—more so in Hawaii than the Galápagos.

White rump patches decorate three types of storm petrels: the **white-vented** or **Eliot's storm petrel** *(Oceanites gracilis);* the nocturnal **Madeiran storm petrel** *(Oceanodroma castro);* and the day-feeding **Galápagos storm petrel** *(Oceanodroma tethys).*

COASTAL BIRDS

While they're not quite as distinctive as their seagoing cousins, the islands' coastal birds make the most of their niche between water and land.

Herons and Egrets

Five species of herons inhabit the islands. All hunt small reptiles, mammals, insects, and fish by waiting motionless, then spearing their prey with a quick jab of their long beaks. The **great blue heron** *(Adrea herodias)* stands 1.5 meters high as it poses one-legged among the mangroves. You might be surprised by one standing silent and fearless in a Puerto Ayora back alley. The smaller **yellow-crowned night heron** *(Nyctanassa violacea)* feeds by night. Its hunched shoulder and furtive, yellow-eyed glance give it a cloak-and-dagger look, capped by a bright yellow sweep of feathers atop the head. Lava rocks hide the small, gray **lava heron** *(Butorides sundevalli)*, the only endemic species of heron. They hunt fish, crabs, and lizards in rocky tide pools.

Greater Flamingos

About 500 of these pink, leggy birds *(Phoenicopters ruber)* wade through brackish lagoons around the archipelago. Punta Cormorant on Floreana, Red Beach on Rabida, and near Dragon Hill on Santa Cruz are good places to see them feeding on brine shrimp by filtering through the salty ooze. Listen closely and you can hear the quiet splooshes as the birds, heads upside-down, push the water through their hairy beak filters similar to whale's baleen. Here's a cocktail-party fact for you: flamingos are actually white, but they turn pink from the carotene pigments in the shrimp they eat.

Waders, Paddlers, and Beach Stalkers

The **American oystercatcher** *(Haematopus ostralegus)* looks like a bad drawing of a bird: head too small, red bill too large. Only 150 or so pairs of these bright-eyed birds live in the islands, where they comb intertidal areas for food. Along with flamingos, inland bodies of water are home to the **white-cheeked pintail duck** *(Anas bahamensis)*, also known as the Bahamas duck, along with the **common stilt** *(Himantopus mexicanus)*.

Galápagos shorelines and beaches are patrolled by **whimbrels** *(Numenius phaeopus)*, **sanderlings** *(Crocethia alba)*, **ruddy turnstones** *(Arenaria interpres)*, **northern phalaropes** *(Lobipes lobatus)*, and **semipalmated plovers** *(Charadrius semipalmatus)*.

LAND BIRDS

The only way that land birds could have reached the Galápagos was to have been blown far out to sea by a storm, which is why only 29 species inhabit the islands today. Those that arrived survived by adapting, eventually dividing into 22 endemic species. A greater variety of the endemic species can be found on islands with higher elevations, which have more vegetation zones, and thus, more ecological niches.

Darwin's Finches

The Galápagos' 13 species of finches, made

famous by Charles Darwin's work, all look more or less alike. Don't worry about trying to tell them apart; just being aware of their significance is enough. After all, as one researcher noted, "it is only a very wise man or a fool who thinks he is able to identify all the finches which he sees."

The key to the finches, as Darwin quickly noticed, is the beak. Different types of finches have beaks of different sizes and shapes, allowing them to gobble many different kinds of food. Short, thick beaks enable **ground finches** to crack hard seeds, whereas longer, slimmer bills allow other species to probe crevices for insects and munch cacti or flowers. The finches, it seems, evolved to fill a wide range of ecological niches left vacant by the lack of other terrestrial birds—a process ecologists call **adaptive radiation.** At the same time, they remained similar enough to have obviously come from a common ancestor. Darwin noticed all this, writing: "The most curious fact is the perfect gradation in the size of the beaks in the different species. One might really fancy that from an original paucity of birds in this archipelago, one species had been taken and modified for different ends."

The eating habits of a few finches are worth special mention. **Woodpecker** and **mangrove finches** use a cactus spine or small twig to get at a fat, tasty grub burrowed deep in a tree branch, making them one of the few animals to use and modify tools. The sharp-billed ground finch goes one step farther—this unremarkable brown bird pecks at the base of a boobie's tail until a trickle of blood starts flowing, which the finch drinks without much protest from its victim. These "vampire finches," as they have been nicknamed, also roll other birds' eggs—some nearly as big as themselves—over lava rocks until they crack, then eat the insides.

Mockingbirds

Like the finches, the four species of mockingbirds endemic to the Galápagos seem to have filled a niche usually taken by other animals. In this case, small land mammals were absent, leaving the mockingbirds free to pick up insects, small reptiles, and various scraps. The birds exhibit an interesting family bonding, in which related groups guard territory and share in the responsibilities of raising juveniles.

The ranges of the four species are separated onto different islands. The **Galápagos mockingbird** *(Nesomimus parvulus)* is the most widespread, found on Isabela, Floreana, Santa Cruz, Santiago, and Santa Fe. San Cristóbal is home to the **Chatham mockingbird** *(Nesomimus melanotis),* and on Española, you'll find the inquisitive **Hood mockingbird** *(Nesomimus macdonaldi),* with its long, curved beak. The **Charles mockingbird** *(Nesomimus trifasciatus)* once ranged over the Floreana area, but today is limited to a few nearby islets.

Other Land Birds

Because it has no natural enemies, the **Galápagos hawk** *(Buteo galapagoensis)* is known for its fearlessness. Darwin noted that "a gun here is almost superfluous; for with the muzzle I pushed a hawk out of the branch of a tree." This endemic scavenger is actually a type of buzzard. Through an unusual mating system known as *cooperative polyandry,* up to four males may mate with a single female and cooperate to help her raise the young, regardless (and ignorant) of whose offspring they are.

It's a tossup as to which land bird is the prettiest. In the running is the **Galápagos dove** *(Zenaida galapagoensis),* whose plumage combines pink, gray, and white with red feet, an aqua-blue eye ring, and green iridescent patches on either side of the neck. Because many of these birds were hunted for food by early visitors, Galápagos doves aren't as tame as they once were, hiding under bushes and eating the opuntia cactus. The male **vermilion flycatcher** *(Pyrocephalus rubinus)* looks like a small fireball in the trees, with its brilliant red coloring set off by a black eye stripe, wing, and tail. It typically catches insects in the highlands, along with the bright **yellow warbler** *(Dendroica petechia),* whose liquid song echoes on most islands.

Early morning and evening are the best times to catch the **short-eared owl** *(Asio flameus)* out after chicks, rodents, and insects. The endemic **Galápagos barn owl** *(Tyto punctissima)* is nocturnal, so there's less chance you'll glimpse this moon-faced bird on the prowl.

Cattle Egrets *(Bubulcus ibis)* have been expanding their range around the globe, and were first reported in Galapagos in 1960. Since then, their numbers have increased. While not introduced by humans, they have spread through the islands, posing a dilemma for scientists and the National Park. Evolution is not static, but this self-introduced species has expanded its range from the agricultural areas, putting pressure on some of the longer-established species.

INSECTS AND ARTHROPODS

Few insects make their home in the Galápagos, because of the islands' isolation and short growing season. Those that do live here are usually dull-colored and come out only at night to escape the heat. As a result, many flowers are light-colored, so their insect pollinators can find them even in low light.

The **carpenter bee** *(Xylocopa darwini)* is one of the most important pollinators in the archipelago. Rocks and sand hide the endemic **Galápagos scorpion** *(Centruroides exsul),* a favorite prey of lava lizards. Also hunted by lava lizards, the bright **painted locust** *(Shistocerca melanocera)* wears a carapace decorated with red, yellow, green, and black. All of these insects are abundant in the lowlands.

FISH

Waters around the Galápagos shelter a strange mix of cold and warm-water species. The variety differs, depending on where and when you're in the water. Currents and seasons bring water as cold as 15°C and as warm as 30°C to the islands, and the waters on different sides of the same island at the same time can vary as much as two–three degrees. Lava rocks serve as aquatic condos in place of coral reefs. Such a wide range of habitats allows more than 300 regular fish species to inhabit the surrounding ocean. Almost one-quarter of these are endemic—every one of the 15 fish Darwin brought back to England was identified as a new species.

Even snorkelers can enjoy a colorful show in the shallows. The **moorish idol** *(Zanclus cornutus)* trails a long dorsal fin over a body banded with black, yellow, and white, and the **blue parrotfish** *(Scarus ghobban)* wears pastel green, blue, and pink. The **harlequin wrasse** *(Bodianus eclancheri)* is one of the most colorful fish around, covered with spatters of orange, red, black, and white. This type of wrasse is called a protogynus hermaphrodite, meaning it can spontaneously change sex from female to male.

Lava rocks hide the **hieroglyphic hawkfish** *(Cirrhitus rivulatus),* colored in complicated patterns of brown, yellow, and gray. It seems as if the **red-lipped batfish** *(Ogcocephalus darwini)* was made from leftover parts, with a forehead horn, long snout, and stiff pectoral fins it uses as makeshift legs. True to its name, the bizarre-looking batfish sports a bright-red mouth and is usually seen on night dives. Even stranger is the mottled **four-eyed blenny** *(Dialommus fuscus),* which can breathe air temporarily as it travels up to 30 meters from the water in search of insects and crabs. Its eyes are each split into two parts, enabling it to see above and below the surface simultaneously.

One of the biggest thrills while diving in the Galápagos is to be engulfed by an opaque school of fish that seems to go on forever—veteran divers describe being blinded by fish for 20 minutes or more. Deep-sea schoolers include **amberjacks** *(Seriola rivoliana),* **yellow-tailed surgeonfish** *(Prionurus laticlavius),* **steel pompanos** *(Trachinotus stilbe),* and **barracudas** *(Sphyraena idiastes).*

Sharks and Rays

Stingrays frequent sandy beaches—your guide should warn you when it's wise to shuffle your feet to keep from stepping on one and getting stung. Formations of **golden rays** *(Rhinoptera steindachneri)* and the beautiful **leopard-spotted eagle ray** *(Aetobatus narinari)* often slip through the shallow waters of mangrove lagoons. These last two, as well as **manta rays** up to six meters across, frequent open water as well.

© JULIAN SMITH

Sally lightfoot crab

White-tipped sharks and **black-tipped sharks** are also seen near shore. Both have dorsal fins tipped with their respective color. Farther out to sea, large schools of **hammerhead sharks** provide divers with enough excitement or terror (or both) for a week of normal diving. **Whale sharks** up to 20 meters long drift after schools of plankton, trailing remoras from their flanks. These last two are most often seen by divers at Wolf and Darwin Islands.

MARINE INVERTEBRATES

No slide show of a Galápagos trip is complete without at least a handful of pictures of the **Sally lightfoot crab** *(Grapsus grapsus)*, which are named for their ability to skip across water for short distances. The crabs' brilliant reds and yellows stand out perfectly against dark volcanic rocks, making for countless photo opportunities.

In shallow waters, snorkelers come across **golden sand dollars** while foraging along sandy bottoms dotted with **pencil-spined sea urchins** and many neon-colored species of **starfish.** Gulf stars have bright red and/or white spiny backs, whereas the blood star is, naturally, pure red. Black sun stars fold their legs under their body during the day, and fragile stars seldom have five legs of equal length.

Many divers consider **scallops** to be the most beautiful marine invertebrate. The 15-centimeter shells of the magnificent scallop *(Lyropecten magnificus)* snap shut when divers approach, so you'll have to sneak up slowly to see the beautiful crimson and violet of the inner mantle, lined with golden tentacles and blue eye spots. **Slipper lobsters** *(Lyropecten magnificus)* venture out at night to avoid predators—an option the heavily hunted and less mobile **sea cucumber** doesn't have.

The waters off the islands are too cold for true reef-building coral, but other types are found in the depths. **Pebble coral** *(Cycloseris mexicana)* lies loose on the bottom beneath masses of endemic **yellow-black coral** *(Antipathes galapagensis).* The electric-orange **cup coral** *(Tubastraea tagusensis)* is thought to have been wiped out by the 1982–1983 El Niño.

On the reefs, you'll find the **leopard-spotted sea anemone** *(Antiparactis)*, along with **golden sea fans** *(Muricea)*, made up of thousands of tiny individual polyps held together by eight arms. In the shadows lurk **squid** and **octopi,** blending in perfectly with their surroundings by expanding and contracting colored skin cells called chromatophores. **Nudibrachs,** shell-less members of the snail family Gastropoda who have taken to the water, come in a range of bright colors. These beautiful floating slugs eat other invertebrates, such as anemones and jellyfish, each of which probably dies surprised that its stinging cells (nematocysts) didn't protect it. The nudibrachs digest their prey and store the stinging cells for their own use later on.

FLORA

"All the plants have a wretched, weedy appearance," wrote Darwin in *The Voyage of the Beagle,* "and I did not see one beautiful flower." Although it may be uninspiring at times, the flora of the Galápagos is worth a second look. True, most of it is desert or semidesert vegetation, and in certain seasons the lower parts of the islands look about as lush as a vacant lot. But they're unique dead-looking plants—of the Galápagos's 550 native species, about 34 percent are endemic (42 percent when all subspecies and varieties are included).

Many species, such as opuntia and *scalesia,* have evolved from a single original colonizer species on one island to more than a dozen species endemic to different islands today. And there are even regions of true, wet green in the upper altitudes of the higher islands, distinguished from their tropical mainland counterparts only by an abundance of endemic species.

Vegetation in the Galápagos is divided into three areas by altitude and climate. The coastal or littoral area that surrounds each shoreline is delimited by the meeting of fresh highland water with oceanic salt water. The semideserts of the dry areas receive the most visitors, whereas the lush, humid area is the smallest, continually dampened by the *garúa* mist.

Coastal Areas

Tangled walls of **mangroves,** ringing many islands like a woody mat of uncombed hair, are good examples of plants' adaptations to salty conditions. Able to grow only in brackish waters, mangroves weave themselves into

the sand and marshes by sending down prop roots from limbs and sending up small breathing roots called *pneumatophores.* Long, pendant seedlings drop into the water, where they either stick vertically into the bottom or float until they lodge somewhere suitable for sprouting.

Mangrove species can usually be distinguished by their leaves. The red mangrove *(Rhizophora mangle)* has larger, pointier, shinier leaves than the white mangrove *(Languncularia racemosa).* Also found in the archipelago are the black mangrove *(Avicennia germinans)* and the less common button mangrove *(Conocarpus erectus).*

The creeping stems of the **beach morning glory** *(Ipomoea pes-caprae)* support the plant's beautiful, funnel-shaped flowers. The lavender blossoms are among the largest in the islands, and the vine is important in stabilizing sands along the coast. The **lava morning glory** *(Ipomoea habeliona)* also has long, tubular blossoms. The fleshy leaves of the **sesuvium** species, common throughout the archipelago, change from bright red in the dry season to green in the wet season. Land iguanas love them, despite their salty taste. Leaves of the **saltbush** *(Cryptocarpus puriformis)* are even brinier.

Dry Areas

Most of the shrubs in this intermediate region are usually prickly and uninviting (the better to ward off predators), and almost all are xerophytic (tolerant of dry conditions). The **palo santo** *(Bursera graveolens)* is the most visible species, blanketing entire hillsides with its lifeless gray forms during the dry season. The tree, a relative of frankincense and myrrh, is burned as incense in churches for its fragrant (and insect-repelling) smoke. Its name, meaning "holy wood," comes from its habit of flowering near Christmas.

The other plants you'll remember best from your visit are the **cacti,** the most distinctive flora of the islands. Like their mainland cousins, Galápagos cacti bristle with protective spines (actually leaves adapted for defense and water retention) and fat stems to store water. The prickly pear cactus *(Opuntia spp.)* provides a lesson in evolution in itself. Fourteen separate species have evolved on different islands from a common ancestor. All have large, flat pads but vary widely in height and armor. On islands with land iguanas and tortoises, the plant's major predators, opuntia have evolved a tall, woody trunk and tough spines for protection. Cacti on Santa Cruz, for example, can grow 12 meters high. On islands with no large predators, on the other hand, opuntia grow low to the ground. These species have spines that are soft enough to allow birds to nest among them—and, with luck, to pollinate the cactus in return.

Other Galápagos cactus species include the endemic lava cactus *(Brachycereus nesioticus)*, a small, chunky plant that's often the first thing to grow in new lava flows, and the candelabra cactus *(Jasminocereus thouarsii)*, whose slim cylindrical trunks can support candlelabra branches up to seven meters across.

Members of the **Scalesia** genus may not be as distinctive as their prickly neighbors, but they've got them beat in diversity, with 15 species and six subspecies spread throughout the islands. The woody shrubs, relatives of the daisy and sunflower, also stem from a single pioneer species and range up into the humid area. The newest species, *Scalesia gordilloi,* was only discovered on Santa Cruz in 1986.

The thorny **palo verde** ("green wood") grows 2–10 meters high. Its scientific name, *Parkinsonia* genus, refers to the plant's tendency to shake like someone with Parkinson's disease during periods of drought. This motion drops the plant's tiny leaves, which would otherwise let too much water evaporate. Four endemic species of **tiquilia** grow low, gray, and ugly in volcanic ash. Even more unappealing is the **amargo** plant *(Castela galapageia)*, a shrub so bitter that even goats won't touch it. The nasty little fruit of the **manzanillo** *(Hippomane mancinella)* is poisonous, and its sap can cause severe skin reactions. Steer clear of this 10-meter-high tree, also called the "poison apple," and its small, green leaves and flowers.

It's hard to believe, but the fruit of the tiny, wild **Galápagos tomato** *(Lycopersicon cheesmanii)* contains about 40 times more vitamin A and beta-carotene than its supermarket cousin. Cross-bred varieties are being developed for commercial distribution.

Humid Areas

The moist highlands of Santiago, Santa Cruz, San Cristóbal, and Floreana support dense forests of **lechoso** *(Scalesia pedunculata)*. Garlands of mosses, ferns, and liverworts festoon the tall trees' branches, along with orchids and clumps of Galápagos mistletoe *(Phoradendron henslovii)*. Some 90 species of **ferns** are found in the higher reaches, including the three-meter fern tree *(Cyathea weatherbyana)* on Santa Cruz.

Cacotillo, or cat's claw *(Miconia robinsonia),* gives its name to a humid area subregion. The shrub, which is endemic to Santa Cruz and San Cristóbal, sports colorful purple and pink flowers. Charles Darwin even had a flower named after him—the tiny white blossoms of the endemic **Darwin's aster** *(Darwiniothamnus tenuifolius)* peek from the highland grasses.

Santa Cruz and Nearby Islands

The geographic and economic center of the Galápagos, Santa Cruz (pop. 12,000) is almost a visit in itself. Actually, if you're short on time or money (or both), that's not a bad idea—much of the island can be seen independently or with a guide hired in Puerto Ayora, and many of the best Galápagos sites are within day-trip range.

PUERTO AYORA AND VICINITY

The largest city in the Galápagos is small by any standards. Brightly colored houses line streets made of sole-scouring volcanic cobblestones, and front yards lined with flowering vines are more likely to have a boat up on blocks than a car. With the highest standard of living in the islands, Puerto Ayora is a tourist

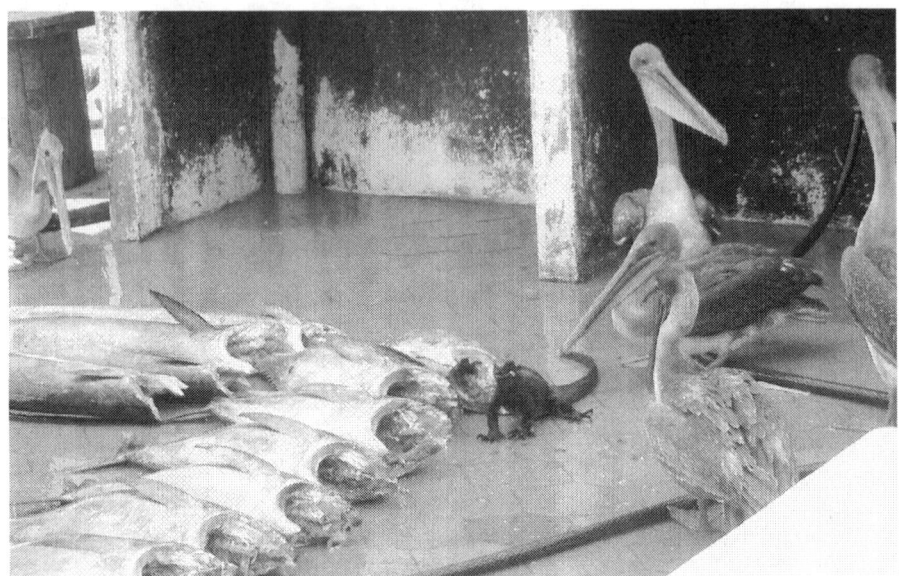

© JEAN BROWN

marine iguana and pelicans checking the quality and freshness of the catch

town where travel agencies, hotels, restaurants, and souvenir stores compete for the flood of dollars released from cruise ships. Everything here is more expensive than on the mainland, especially film, food, and batteries. Residents will tell you that the only things lacking on Puerto Ayora are enough fresh water and a good hospital (most medical emergencies are handled in Quito).

Entertainment and Events

La Panga downstairs and **Bongo Bar** upstairs don't complete with the Seventh Day Adventist church next door on the bend in Charles Darwin. A handful of mellower bars are scattered around town; try **Limón y Café,** on the corner of Darwin and 12 de Febrero.

Shopping

Throw a rock in the air in Puerto Ayora, and you'll probably hit a T-shirt or souvenir stand. There has to be a shop in Puerto Ayora named after every animal in the Galápagos.

Most sell stamps, postcards, and T-shirts and offer mail services, but for the last, the post office is more dependable—plus, collectors can sometimes obtain colorful stamps with Galápagos themes. A few shops have book exchanges. Remember to steer clear of buying anything made of endangered black coral or shells.

The Charles Darwin Center has two good gift shops whose profits go to the National Park and the Darwin Foundation. The **Galápagos Gallery** has a high-quality selection of souvenirs, including many wood carvings.

Recreation and Tours

Snorkeling gear is available for rent on almost every corner, but the best equipment comes from the dive shops. Book local snorkeling trips on a glass-bottomed boat with **Aqua Tours** (tel. 2/252-6234). Two good spots in Darwin Bay are Las Grietas, across from the docks, and off the beach near the Charles Darwin Research Center (watch for *pangas*).

PUERTO AYORA

Rent bicycles from $12 per day at several agencies.

The **Moonrise Travel Agency** (tel. 5/252-6403, yennydivine@hotmail.com) is great for last-minute bookings aboard boats in the area. Tours of four to eight days are available, and day tours to Santa Fé, South Plaza, Seymour Norte, and Bartolomé are available from $65 pp per day. **Galaven** (tel. 5/252-6359) operates the *Galápagos Adventure I* and *II* and the *Esmeraldas III* for day tours. Guayaquil-based **Galasam** (tel. 5/252-6126) owns several boats and has a helpful office staff. **Gala Travel** (tel. 5/252-6581) runs mostly smaller economy boats. All are on Darwin near the town park.

Accommodations

Most of Puerto Ayora's budget hotels are afflicted with brackish water, and many don't have hot water. A friendly family runs the **Bed and Breakfast Peregrina** (Darwin and Indefategable, tel. 5/252-6323) out of their home. Five rooms with private baths run $22 pp, including breakfast. There's a shady terrace and garden, and laundry service is available.

Los Amigos (Darwin and 12 de Febrero, tel. 5/252-6265) has rooms with shared bath for $15 s, $20 d. The small, friendly **Hotel Santa Cruz** (Baltra and Indefategable) has six rooms with shared bath for $10 pp. The **Hotel Salinas** (Naveda and Berlanga, tel./fax 5/252-6107) is central and clean, with a small garden, communal cable TV, a restaurant, and rooms for $35 with private bath. Rooms at the recently upgraded **Lobo de Mar** (12 de Febrero and Darwin, tel. 5/252-6188, fax 5/252-6569) are $75 s, $99 d, with private bath, air-conditioning, and balconies.

Forty dollars will get you a single with private bath and hot water at the **Hotel Castro** (Los Colonos and Malecón, tel. 5/256-5089, fax 5/252-6113, $60 d). It's recommended as a clean, quiet place with fans, a terrace, a restaurant, and a bar. The **Estrella del Mar,** around the corner on 12 de Febrero (tel. 5/252-6427, $46 s, $66 d), is often recommended for its ocean views. Several new hotels have opened and others have been remodeled, mostly within one or two blocks of Charles Darwin. They are all in the $80–130 price range. To find a double, look for **Fernandina, Fiesta, Mainao** and **Red Booby.**

Muted orange path lights lead you through the mangroves to the **Red Mangrove Inn** (Darwin and Las Fragatas, tel./fax 5/252-6564, info@redmangrove.com, www.redmangrove .com), the hippest place in the islands. Opened in late 1994, this small hotel is as cozy as a California artist's weekend home (no shoes inside), with wine bottles in the walls decorated with batiks and tiles made by one of the previous owners. The dining room opens onto a deck and hot tub overlooking Darwin Bay. Rooms at the Red Mangrove cost $125–260 s, $155–290 d, with mountain bikes, sea kayaks, and windsurfing equipment available on request. The owners also offer tours of Santa Cruz by mountain bike, kayak, and horseback. The restaurant Red Sushi has you-know-what, plus other seafood dishes.

Behind El Pelicano restaurant sits the ◖ **Hotel Silberstein** (Darwin and Los Piqueros, tel./fax 5/252-6277, $100 s, $180 d), a beautiful place surrounding a tropical courtyard. Every spacious room has a fan and private bath with solar-heated water, and those on the second floor open onto terraces over the swimming pool. The owners speak Spanish, English, and German and can arrange day tours.

Angermeyer's Waterfront Inn is the latest addition to gracious living. Accessed by water taxi near Angermeyer's Point, it was the home of Gus Angermeyer and has been fully

Angermeyer's Point

remodeled by his son Teppy into a lovely, spacious hotel overlooking the bay. Prices for doubles with breakfast range $134–218, plus tax.

A water taxi and short walk from town is the recently remodeled (**Finch Bay Eco Hotel** (tel. 2/250-8810, ext. 2810, www.ecuadorable.com, $250 d), one of the plushest options around. The 21 rooms have soft beds, and guests can enjoy a secluded beach for sunbathing, and snorkeling. Also in the highlands is the (**Hotel Royal Palm Galápagos** (tel./fax 5/252-7408, info@royalpalmgalapagos.com, www.royalpalmhotel.net), a palatial spread with 10 villas, four veranda studios, and three suites, all with satellite TV, Internet access, and sweeping views of the highlands. There's a fine-dining restaurant and a piano bar, and for fun a pool, spa, gym, and tennis courts. Prices start at $420 per night.

Food

Start your day off with a filling traditional breakfast of *bolon,* eggs, beef stew, and juice or coffee—or just a regular American breakfast—at the **Descanso del Guia** on Darwin. It also has good, inexpensive set lunches. Several small kiosks along Binford east of Baltra are open in the evening (and some in the afternoons), serving traditional dishes that are prepared well and served fresh and cheap. The **Kiosco William** offers tasty *encocado de langostino* (lobster in coconut sauce).

On the corner of Darwin and Binford, the **Tropicbird Cafe** (next to Moonrise travel agency) is perfect for people-watching. Homemade cakes and breads are on the menu, with sandwiches and salads for $5–11. The **Hernan Café Bar Rest** facing the park has two open-walled bars, walls of lava stone, and lamps made of dried cacti. Breakfast is $3.50–5.50, pizzas are $6 and up, and pasta, fish, and meat dishes are $6–12. Coffee drinks cost $2–4.

I like **La Dolce Italia:** it's air-conditioned, and pasta dishes such as spaghetti puttanesca with fish and black olives are $6–11. **Tintorera** (Floreana and Darwin) serves good breakfasts and organic salads starting around $4–12. Try

the cakes and fruit pies. **Café de Mar,** up the block, offers good pies (which sell out quickly). Sandwiches are $5 and up, and pizzas range $6–20. **The Rock** (Darwin and Naveda) is the new place to eat. Friday night is sushi night, and its tasty lunches and dinners keep the crowds coming.

For seafood, try (**Restaurant Salvavidas** by the docks, the most authentically nautical in decor and location. It's popular with tourists and locals alike, who will tell you it's the best seafood place in town. Fish dishes are good and inexpensive, starting around $4.50. The open-air tables at (**La Garrapata** are always packed after sundown, because it's the longest-running quality restaurant in Puerto Ayora. Good music and an attractive setting go well with the excellent *parillada de pescado.* Lunches are $4, à la carte dishes run $7–15, and it has great fresh juice and occasional live music in the evenings.

Angermeyer's Point may not have air-conditioning, but it's got sea breezes, an unbeatable position, and excellent food. Take a water taxi for a romantic fairy-lit supper, or join the "get away from the crowd" lunchers for a seafood feast.

Information and Services

Steer your tourist questions to the **Cámara de Turismo** (Darwin and Binford, tel. 5/252-6206) or the **Galápagos National Park Office** (tel. 5/252-6511) near the Darwin station. Both offer maps and information in English.

Puerto Ayora's **Banco del Pacífico** is probably one of the few in the country that actually overlooks the Pacific. It changes travelers' checks, but lines are often long. Internet access is available around town, but it's slow. Both **Porta** and **Movistar** offer cell phone coverage in much of the islands.

Monyfri Laundry, on 12 Noviembre next to Hotel Fernandina, will get your togs clean and dry in a few hours for $0.75 a pound.

Transportation

CITEG and **Transgalapagos,** both based at the new bus terminal, send eight buses to

© JULIAN SMITH

Marine iguanas claim a dock in Puerto Ayora, on Santa Cruz Island.

the airport between 6:30 and 9:45 A.M. The whole trip costs $1.80 pp each way and is much quicker now that the road has been paved. Buses can stop on the way out of town anywhere in the highlands, but they're often full coming back from the airport.

The interisland boat service is a series of "Fibras" departing in front of Restaurante Salvavidas at 2 P.M., making the trip ($30 one-way) to Puerto Baquerizo Moreno on Santa Cruz or Puerto Villamil on Isabela. The ride can be quite rough for those prone to seasickness.

Camionetas (pickup trucks) are available for hire all around town; most destinations are $1. **Water taxis** wait at the dock to shuttle passengers to boats waiting in the harbor ($0.60 pp by day, $1 at night). Just go down to the dock, yell "Taxi!" and tell the pilot which boat you're on. You can also wave down taxis from your boat to go into town, or call on radio channel 14.

Interisland flights with **EMETEBE** (Los Colonos and Darwin, tel. 5/252-5177) can get you to Isabela or San Cristóbal in half an hour for $90–100 pp each. The office is on the top

floor overlooking the harbor, in what could pass for a control tower. **TAME** has an office at Darwin and 12 de Febrero (tel. 5/252-6165), and **Aerogal** (tel. 5/244-1950) has an office at Rodrigues Lara and San Cristobal.

Tortuga Bay

One of the most beautiful beaches in the Galápagos is a 45-minute walk from Puerto Ayora. Take Binford out of town to the west, up the steps, and past the National Park guard post. Follow the moderately rough trail straight to the beach. Tortuga Bay beach is wide, flat, and usually empty, and around the iguana-patrolled rocky point is a calm mangrove inlet that's perfect for swimming.

◖ Charles Darwin Research Center

The main arm of the Charles Darwin Foundation for the Galápagos, the Darwin Center (tel. 5/252-6146, info@darwinfoundation.org, www.darwinfoundation.org, 7 A.M.–6 P.M. daily) was begun in the 1960s as a research and breeding center for endangered native species. It's on every tour itinerary.

The visiting area includes the tortoise breeding and rearing center, where endangered subspecies are hatched and cared for until they're old enough to protect themselves in the wild. The program started in 1965 with the Pinzón island tortoise, and it has since expanded with the aim of reproducing 50 of each subspecies each year.

Lonesome George, the last surviving member of the Pinta Island subspecies *(Geochelone elephantopus abindoni)*, has been the most famous resident of the center since he arrived in 1971. Find a female Pinta tortoise and claim the $10,000 reward that's still standing. In August 2008, eggs that appear to be fertile were recovered from Lonesome George's corral, which he inhabits with two females of closely related species. This has aroused great excitement in the scientists at the research center. Farther down the trails are research facilities and offices, near an iguana rearing center that's closed to the public because of the animals' shyness. A beach is open 7 A.M.–6 P.M. daily.

For those interested in keeping up with events on the islands, the foundation publishes the *Galápagos Bulletin* twice a year. Check the website for information on volunteer opportunities.

SANTA CRUZ HIGHLANDS

Because 100 meters of altitude difference in the Galápagos has the same effect on the vegetation as a 600-to-700-meter variance on the mainland, your surroundings change quickly as you climb into the heights of Santa Cruz. Before you know it, you've left the dry, rocky coast for misty forests edging up against fields and pastures.

Seven kilometers above Puerto Ayora are the small towns of **Bellavista** and **Santa Rosa,** from which several trails lead into the hills. The peaks of **Media Luna**, five kilometers from Bellavista, can be climbed in four–five hours, and three kilometers beyond it is **Cerro Crocker,** a journey of seven–eight hours. Guides are advised, but not required.

You can also visit two sets of **lava tunnels** near Bellavista, one called the "Tunnel of Love" for the heart-shaped hole in its ceiling.

© JULIAN SMITH

Galápagos tortoises at Charles Darwin Research Center

Entered through collapsed roof sections, the tunnels stretch into the earth wide enough to drive a semitrailer into and sometimes continue for miles. Admission is charged to enter the tunnels, which are on private land.

Steve Devine's Butterfly Farm, between Bellavista and Santa Rosa, is another regular stop on tours of the highlands. The combination cattle ranch/restaurant offers lunch and dinner with prior notice and has camping spaces. Giant tortoises graze in the wet grass among the cattle, while pure white cattle egrets *(Bubulcus ibis)* strike at bugs like feathered serpents. The tortoises plod through here from the tortoise reserve to the southwest, giving visitors perhaps their only chance to see the giant reptiles in a semi-wild setting. Yellow warblers follow the tortoises picking off parasites, and vermillion flycatchers frequent the trees.

The **El Chato Tortoise Reserve** claims the entire southeast corner of Santa Cruz Island as a habitat for the endemic giant tortoise subspecies. The seven-kilometer journey from **Santa Rosa** can be made by foot or horse. Up the road from Santa Rosa are **Los Gemelos**, twin pit craters formed when large caverns left empty by flowing lava collapsed on themselves. Galápagos hawks, barn owls, and vermillion flycatchers flit through the damp *scalesia* forests surrounding the craters, which lie just off the road to Baltra, a few kilometers past Santa Rosa.

OTHER SANTA CRUZ VISITORS SITES

Bachas Beach

Named for the remains of some wrecked WWII barges that have all but rusted away, this is one of the first sites most cruisers visit. The white-sand beach is a sea turtle nesting site, and at certain seasons, it attracts marauding frigatebirds looking for hatchlings for breakfast, lunch, or supper. The lagoons behind the beach are home to many flamingos, and marine iguanas and sea lions laze around near the waterline.

Black Turtle Cove

Just west of the Canal de Itabaca between Santa Cruz and Baltra, this shallow mangrove lagoon

a *panga* ride among the mangroves in Black Turtle Cove, Santa Cruz

extends far inland. The visit is just a slow *panga* float, leaving you free to admire the abundant birdlife. Lava and great blue herons, lava gulls, frigatebirds, and boobies all nest in the tangled branches of red and white mangroves.

Life beneath the surface is just as active. Spotted eagles and golden rays glide by in slow, silent formation, and a watery snuff sound alerts you to green sea turtles coming up to breathe. Pencil-spined sea urchins and starfish litter the bottom near a shallow rocky neck—navigable only by small craft—where white-tipped sharks sleep swimming against the current.

Cerro Dragon

This new visitor site on the west side of the island has a dry or wet landing, depending on the tide. Within the first few minutes of landing, you'll pass blue-footed boobies propped on the rocks, marine iguanas sunning themselves on the beach, and two lagoons that, depending on the season, may be filled with flamingos. The two-kilometer trail eventually leads to the top of Cerro Dragon, a modest climb with good views, which is named for the land iguanas that congregate nearby.

DAPHNE MAJOR

Biologist Peter Grant spent decades studying finches' beak adaptations on Daphne Major, one half of a pair of tiny islands between Santa Cruz and Santiago. The results, which are considered the first measured study of evolution in action, are described in his book *Beak of the Finch*. Daphne Minor is closed to the public, and visits to Daphne Major (considered a scientific research area more than a visitor site) are strictly limited by the Galápagos National Park Service.

If you're one of the select few visitors, a difficult dry landing will lead you to a steep trail up to the rim of one of the island's two sunken craters. Masked boobies nest on the way up, and blue-footed boobies can be seen inside the crater. The trail continues along the rim to the lip of the second crater, with red-billed tropicbirds visible along the way.

SANTA FÉ

A short sail from Puerto Ayora (two hours) or Puerto Baquerizo Moreno on San Cristóbal (three hours) brings you to the beautiful anchorage off Santa Fé, a shallow bay where

opunita cactus, a favorite food of land tortoises

sea turtles and manta rays are dark shadows against the sandy bottom. After a wet landing, you'll begin a short loop trail starring a local variety of land iguanas. Members of this endemic species are pale yellow with well-defined scales and can grow more than 1.5 meters long. Santa Fé's species of opuntia cactus have grown up to 10 meters high and developed tough, woody stems for defense. Galapagos hawks often sit in the cactus forest, watching and waiting for a meal to present itself.

SEYMOUR NORTE

Volcanic uplift raised this small dot at the end of Baltra. It's a small, crowded island with a loop trail reached by a tricky dry landing. Walking the trail takes 1–2 hours, winding through gray groves of palo santo and opuntia cactus set low to the ground. Because many day trips from Santa Cruz come here, the island can become crowded with people.

Swallow-tailed gulls nest in the rocks near the landing, often with fuzzy chicks. A large colony of blue-footed boobies nests along

the inland part of the loop. Magnificent frigatebirds, part of the largest colony in the Galápagos, nest farther in. At just about any time during the year, you can see the males displaying their bright red air sacs and chattering seductively to females soaring overhead. Marine iguanas and sea lions have claimed the beach along the coastal section of the walk.

SOUTH PLAZA

Just off the east coast of Santa Cruz, a pair of tiny uplift islands curve toward each other like parentheses. At only two square kilometers, South Plaza is one of the smallest islands you'll visit. The distinctive bright yellow of the local land iguanas stands out among the cacti, as the lizards feed on cactus fruit and opuntia pads.

The loop trail begins near one of the largest sea lion colonies in the Galápagos—about 1,000 individuals—and climbs through a surprisingly colorful landscape. During the dry season, South Plaza's *sesuvium* turns bright red, contrasting with the gray and white rocks, green cacti, and turquoise ocean. (The plants become bright green during the rainy season.) Birds barnstorm the cliffs at the far end of the trail, sometimes trying to land three or four times before finally hitting the nest. Audubon's shearwaters, red-billed tropicbirds, boobies, frigatebirds, and swallow-tailed gulls all live near South Plaza's cliffside.

photographing sea lions on Seymour Norte

San Cristóbal

Nothing could be less inviting than the first appearance. A broken field of black basaltic lava, thrown into the most rugged waves, and crossed by great fissures, is every where covered by stunted, sunburnt brushwood, which shows little signs of life.

– Charles Darwin,
The Voyage of the Beagle

Darwin must have landed on San Cristóbal near its northern end, an area covered by lava and eroded volcanoes that give it away as one of the oldest islands in the archipelago. The bottom half of this easternmost island in the Galápagos shelters the provincial capital, Puerto Baquerizo Moreno, below green highland slopes and a freshwater lake.

HISTORY

Near the end of the 19th century, Ecuadorian entrepreneur Manuel J. Cobos began a penal colony in the San Cristóbal highlands. The brutal settlement, named El Progreso (Progress), was intended to make money from sugarcane harvesting, but 14-hour workdays starting at 4 A.M. soon took their toll. For the slightest offense, the 400 prisoners were lashed, executed, or marooned on deserted islands. The penal colony ended in an uprising in 1904. Cobos, who was 67 years old, was shot dead while standing on a porch in his underwear.

Six decades later, a group of more than 100 people from the northwestern United States tried to found a utopian fishing community near Puerto Baquerizo Moreno. The ill-conceived project collapsed within 14 months from a combination of disease, lack of skill, and poor planning. A scheme to catch lobsters and sell them to the U.S. market failed when it was discovered that no one knew how to catch the spiny crustaceans, which were in short supply to begin with.

PUERTO BAQUERIZO MORENO

The capital of the Galápagos Islands is smaller and poorer than Puerto Ayora. It's also less dependent on tourist dollars, because most of the populace fishes for a living or administrates in one of the government offices. Sea lions sleep on dinghies at anchor in the amazingly clear harbor. Prices are generally lower here than in Puerto Ayora.

Sights

The high point of any visit to Baquerizo Moreno is a stop at the town's **Interpretation Center** (tel. 5/252-0358, 7 A.M.–5 P.M. daily, free) down Alsacio Northia past the Cabañas de Don Jorge. It's better than anything in Puerto Ayora outside the Darwin Center, with views of the ocean, wooden walkways, and exhibits on the human and geological history of the islands and, of course, the plants and animals.

Giant windmills adorn a south facing hill in the highlands and generate 60 percent of the

© JEAN BROWN

traditional wooden house in Puerto Baquerizo Moreno

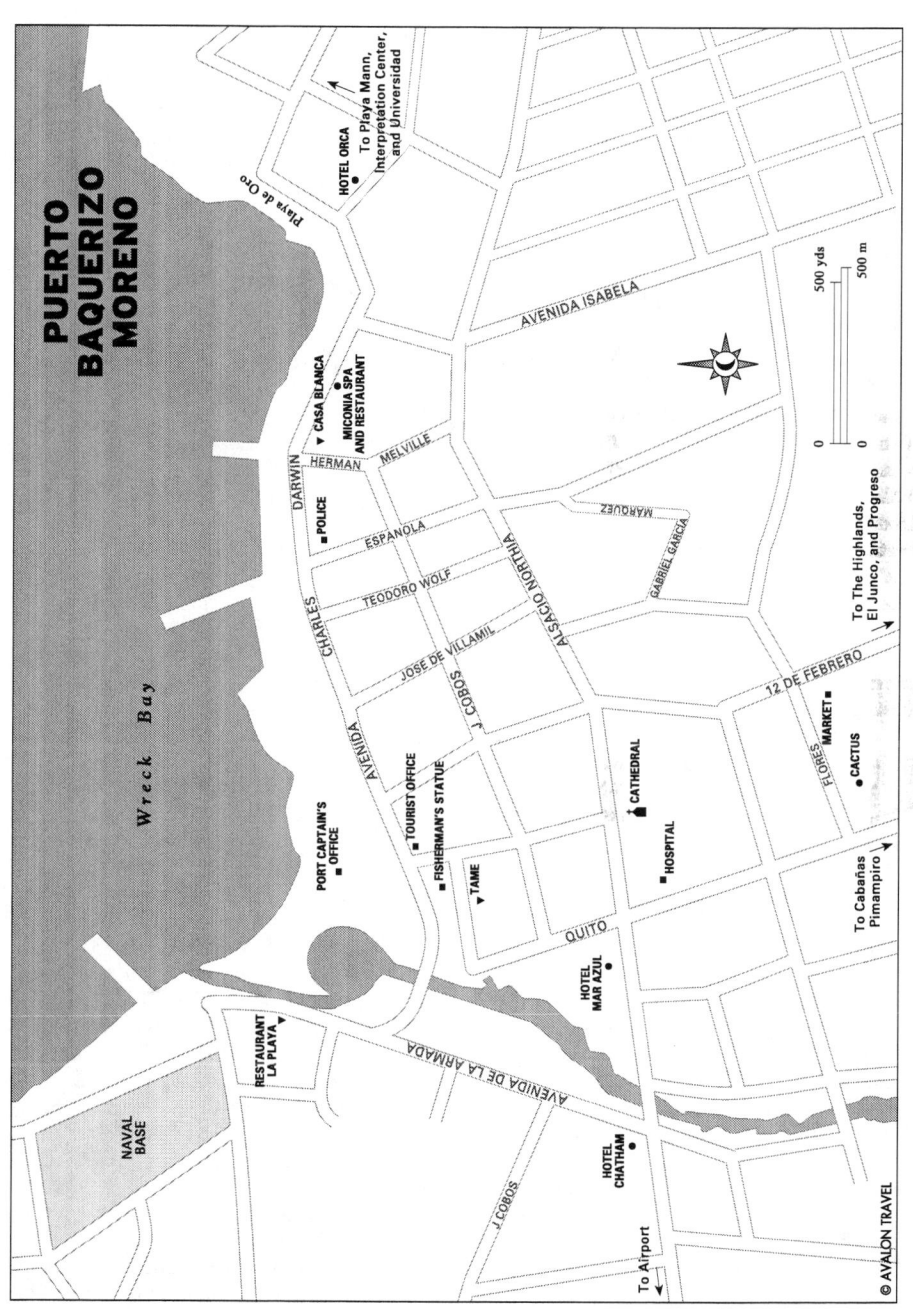

PUERTO BAQUERIZO MORENO

Wreck Bay

Playa de Oro

To Playa Mann, Interpretation Center, and Universidad

HOTEL ORCA

CASA BLANCA
MICONIA SPA AND RESTAURANT

AVENIDA ISABELA

DARWIN
HERMAN
MELVILLE
POLICE
ESPAÑOLA
TEODORO WOLF
JOSE DE VILLAMIL
CHARLES
AVENIDA
ALSACIO NORTHIA
MARQUEZ
GABRIEL GARCÍA
J. COBOS

To The Highlands, El Junco, and Progreso

12 DE FEBRERO
FLORES
MARKET
CACTUS

PORT CAPTAIN'S OFFICE
TOURIST OFFICE
FISHERMAN'S STATUE
TAME
CATHEDRAL
HOSPITAL

QUITO

HOTEL MAR AZUL

To Cabañas Pimampiro

RESTAURANT LA PLAYA

NAVAL BASE

AVENIDA DE LA ARMADA

J. COBOS

HOTEL CHATHAM

To Airport

500 yds
500 m
0
0

© AVALON TRAVEL

© JEAN BROWN

Interpretation Center on San Cristóbal

island's electricity, part of the plan to make use of renewable resources and cut the quantity of diesel being imported into the islands.

Entertainment

Baquerizo Moreno by night features drinks at the **Scuba Bar,** near the pier; and music and board games at **Iguana Rock,** on Juan José Flores near Quito.

Recreation and Tours

Sharksky (tel. 5/252-0349) is open daily and seems to be where the action is. The proprietors have a small café on the Malecón and offer day tours, diving, bike rental, snorkel equipment, surfboards. All prices are competitive.

Chalo's Tours (tel. 5/252-0953) rents diving and snorkeling equipment, mountain bikes, and surfboards. It can organize day tours of the highlands ($25 pp), Playa Chino ($30 pp), Leon Dormida and Isla Lobos ($45 pp), and Punta Pitt and the Galapaguera ($75 pp).

You can reach **Playa Mann** in less than 10 minutes by foot; it's north of town near the interpretation center. **Playa Punta Carola** is 15 minutes past the lighthouse to the north. To reach **Frigatebird Hill,** pass the Cabañas Don Jorge and the University San Francisco, then

turn right through the stone wall near the end of the road after about five minutes. It should take about half an hour to reach the top of the hill from here, and once you get your breath back at the top, you'll be rewarded with views of beaches, bays, cliffs, and the town below. Magnificent and great frigatebirds both nest here at certain times of year.

Accommodations

On the road to the airport **Hotel Chatham** (Northia and Armada Nacional, tel./fax 5/252-0137, chathamhotel@hotmail.com) has rooms with fan, hot water, TV, private bath, and a small pool, starting at $15 pp. The **Islas Galapagos** (Esmeraldas and Colon, tel. 5/252-0203) is newer and also clean. Rooms with the same amenities (except TVs) are $20 s, $30 d. The friendly folks at **Los Cactus** (near the telephone office at Juan José Flores and Quito, tel. 5/252-0078) have 13 rooms with private bath, hot water, and fan for $15 s, $20 d. There are several family-run bed-and-breakfast places—ask for information upstairs at Casa Blanca. Prices are around $15 pp with breakfast.

Baquerizo Moreno's most distinctive accommodations are at the family-run **Cabanas Don**

© JEAN BROWN

Playa Mann is close to town and popular on Sundays.

Jorge (tel. 5/252-0208, cabanasdonjorge@ hotmail.com), on Alsacio Northia east of town. Four unusual cabins have lava-stone walls, high ceilings, bunk beds, and lofts, and one has a fridge and kitchenette. Each cabin also has a fan and a private bath with hot water. Rates are $25 pp and monthly rates run around $550, not including food—in high season, they don't offer short-term rentals. An eating area, bar, and living room fill the main house.

Miconia, along the north end of the Malecón, is the best in town at $59 s, $85 d. Breakfast and use of the spa and gym are included. The restaurant of the same name on the ground floor is open all day except Sundays, when it opens only for dinner.

Overlooking the town are the **Cabanas Pimampiro** (Quito and Tulcan tel. 5/252-0323), with three cabins and three family suites around the pool. Prices start at $60–98, including breakfast.

Food

Grab a quick snack and a drink on the outdoor patio of **Casa Blanca,** beyond the Pocita at the shorter pier. For dependable lunches, locals head to **Perla Pacífico** (Villamil and Charles Darwin) and the **Cebichería El Langostino**

(Melville and Hernandez). Rustic **Albacora** (Northia and Española) is recommended by locals for its seafood and big breakfasts; generous *platos* run $4–6.

A favorite of the international yacht crowd, **Restaurant Rosita** (Hernandez and Villamil) has been around for 50 years. It has lots of character and an extensive menu, with set meals around $3. **La Playa,** close to the entrance to the naval base, is popular with tourists and locals for a special supper.

Information and Services

There's a **CAPTURGAL** tourist information office (tel. 5/252-1124, 8 A.M.–noon and 2–5:30 P.M. Mon.–Fri.) on Darwin near Wolf, and telephone cabins at several locations. The **post office** is at the western end of Darwin, past the Municipal Building.

Transportation

Buses leave from the Malecón half a dozen times daily for El Progreso in the highlands. **Taxis** to El Progreso cost about $3. The interisland boat service departs at 7 A.M. each morning to Santa Cruz ($30 pp); for Isabela, continue from Santa Cruz after lunch for another $30 pp.

© JEAN BROWN

pink flamingo at San Cristóbal's airport

EMETEBE (tel./fax 5/252-0036) has flights leaving most mornings at 8 A.M. for Baltra ($90 pp one-way, 30 minutes) and Isabela ($100 pp, 45 minutes). San Cristóbal's **airport** is at the end of Alsacio Northia past the radio station.

SAN CRISTÓBAL HIGHLANDS

You don't need to be part of a tour group to visit San Cristóbal's highlands, although it does occasionally help with transportation. Avenida 12 de Febrero climbs north out of Baquerizo Moreno to El Progreso, a notorious former penal colony that's now a quiet farming village. Here you'll find the **Casa del Ceibo** (tel. 5/252-0248), a house in a huge ceibo tree that you can rent for $15 pp per night. You'll have to provide your own food, but it's a good way to avoid the heat of the lowlands. The casa offers *parilladas* and other typical foods on weekends. The **Quinta D'Cristhi** also has food on weekends, along with football and volleyball games.

Tracks continue north from here to the

settlement of Soledad, near an overlook at the southern end of the island, and east to Cerro Verde and Los Arroyos. On the way to Cerro Verde is the **Laguna El Junco,** one of the few freshwater lakes in the islands. The collapsed caldera is fed by rainwater, and it shelters wading birds and seven species of Darwin's finches. El Junco is 10 kilometers past El Progreso; follow the highway and take a right onto a steep dirt track to get there. A narrow trail encircles the rim, offering views of almost the entire island.

Trails continue from Cerro Verde along the length of the island. Destinations include **Puerto Chino,** a beach on the south coast 30 minutes downhill; **La Galapaguera** to the north, where San Cristóbal tortoises reside in the wild; and **Hobbs Bay** and **Punta Pitt** at the far north end of the island. The southbound track near El Junco leads to Jatun Sacha's center where volunteers can live and work eradicating invasive (unwanted) plant species and replant with native endemics.

OTHER VISITORS SITES

All sites on San Cristóbal are within day-trip range of Puerto Baquerizo Moreno. Around the western point of the island, directly south of the airport, is **La Lobería.** Half an hour by boat will bring you within sight of sea lions, blue-footed boobies, and the endemic San Cristóbal mockingbird. It's possible to walk here from Baquerizo Moreno in half an hour, or you can hire a taxi. **Isla Lobos,** 30 minutes north of Baquerizo Moreno by boat, also takes its name from sea lions. Blue-footed boobies nest on the tiny islet, but because the dry landing and hike are both difficult, the site is not that popular.

Visits to sites on San Cristóbal's north coast are often combined with a stop at one of the beaches near Isla Lobos, including **Playa Ochoa, El Muerto,** and **Playa El Manglesito.** Farther north is **Puerto Grande** (also called Sapho Cove), a beach facing one of the Galápagos's most famous

© JEAN BROWN

Kayaks provide a quiet ride in the bay.

landmarks, **Kicker Rock.** Called León Dormido (Sleeping Lion) in Spanish, this leaning bolt of volcanic tuff stands 146 meters high a short distance from the coast. If your captain feels adventurous and sails through a narrow split in the rock, you'll see blue-footed and masked boobies nesting near frigatebirds on the rocks.

Just past Kicker Rock, the beach at **Cerro Brujo** provides a relaxing stop of swimming and snorkeling. The northeastern tip of San Cristóbal is named **Punta Pitt,** where a great visitors site was opened in 1989. A wet landing and long hike bring you inland to the only place you can see red-footed boobies in the Galápagos besides Tower Island. Other seabirds find the spot equally enticing, including masked and blue-footed boobies, frigatebirds, storm petrels, and swallow-tailed gulls.

Santiago and Nearby Islands

SANTIAGO
The Galápagos's fourth-largest island once had the distinction of harboring one of the archipelago's largest and most destructive herds of feral goats. The four goats left on the island in the early 1800s multiplied to more than 100,000 by the middle of the 20th century. Recent backbreaking efforts by the Park Service and the Charles Darwin Research Center reduced the population, and in 2006 goats were successfully eradicated.

Sullivan Bay
This site on the east end of Santiago near Bartolomé sounds like one of the dullest—an hour-long walk over bare lava—but it can be one of the most enchanting. An eruption in 1897 left the area covered in mesmerizing patterns of black lava. Frozen blorps and squirts punctuate the endless expanse of smoky chaos frozen in stone, which is rough on the shoes but captivating to the eyes. The lava's glassy, almost ceramic feel comes from its high silicate

content. This may have been one place Darwin had in mind when he wrote, ". . . immense deluges of black, naked lava, which have flowed either over the rims of the great caldrons, like pitch over the rim of a pot in which it has been boiled, or have burst forth from smaller orifices on the flanks."

Buccaneer Cove

A freshwater source just inland made this cove a haven for pirates during the 17th and 18th centuries. Today, tour boats sail past under impressive cliff faces spotted with a millennia's worth of guano from nesting birds and dark volcanic sand beaches lead to hillsides.

James Bay

An easy wet landing sets you on the black beach of **Puerto Egas,** home to a dozing posse of sea lions. Snorkelers will enjoy exploring the rocks to the right. A two-kilometer, three-hour loop trail leads inland past the rusted remains of a 1960s salt operation. Cruise-ship crews have built a makeshift soccer field nearby. (Your guide might tell you about a National Park guard who was forgotten here in the 1950s for nearly eight months, instead of the usual three—legend has it that he was taken off the island in a straitjacket.) Overhead soar Galápagos hawks, while on the ground, you may spot Galápagos doves, mockingbirds, and even a Galápagos scorpion under a rock.

Farther down the trail are the famous fur-seal grottoes, where the heaving ocean fills a series of pools and underwater caverns that are occupied by seals, sea lions, and crabs. It's a shame that visitors are no longer allowed to swim here, although it's understandable: the long trail is often crowded with as many as six tour groups at once. A wealth of marine life teems in the tidal pools. Bright Sally lightfoot crabs crawl over marine iguanas the color of lava, and yellow-crowned night herons, oystercatchers, and sandpipers hunt among the crevices. Four-eyed blennies and numerous marine invertebrates lurk underwater. Lavender sea-

wave-sculpted scenery at James Bay, Santiago

© JULIAN SMITH

urchin spines blanket the beach near the end of the trail.

A second, little-used path from the landing ascends **Sugarloaf Volcano,** about 1,000 feet high. **Espumilla Beach,** a second beach slightly north of Puerto Egas, is the start of a trail through mangroves to a lagoon populated by Galápagos flamingos and other wading birds. Sea turtles nest on the sand near the mangroves, and snorkeling and swimming off the wide beach are possible.

BARTOLOMÉ ISLAND

Most boats anchor under Pinnacle Rock on the southwestern end of Bartolomé Island. From here, it's a short *panga* ride to the mangrove-fringed beach, one of the island's two visitor sites. This is a relatively relaxed site—most guides will let you do your own thing for an hour or two, then herd everyone on to the climb. Don't miss this chance to snorkel: In addition to hosting the usual spectacular underwater sights, this is one of your best opportunities to swim with Galápagos penguins. Keep your eyes open, and you'll probably see one of the stubby black torpedoes shooting past after a school of fish. It may not be able to fly, but the Galápagos penguin sure can swim—at speeds up to 40 kilometers per hour.

Back on shore, a trail heads through the mangroves to a beach on the other side of the neck. You can't swim off this beach (white-tipped sharks and stingrays aplenty), but between December and March, you may glimpse female sea turtles waiting for night to come ashore and lay their eggs. Birders should keep their eyes open for Galápagos hawks, herons, and oystercatchers near the mangroves.

The other site on Bartolomé begins with a tricky dry landing on a rock jetty that is usually guarded by sea lions, sleeping as often as not. The 30-minute climb to the top of the island is made easier by a wooden staircase winding up the blasted volcanic face. It's a real moonscape up here, scarred by lava chutes and parasitic spatter cones (offshoots of the main lava tube).

The incredibly light lava rocks come in a rainbow of pastel colors, from creams, grays, and browns to almost floral hues of rose and lime. Pioneer species such as *tiquilia* and lava cactus are only beginning to gain a foothold on the jagged landscape.

The famous view from the 108-meter summit is worth the hot climb. In front of you stretches the neck of Bartolomé, green with mangroves and punctuated by 40-meter Pinnacle Rock. Santiago Island covers most of the horizon—notice the Sullivan Bay lava flow to the left and how it enveloped offshore islands like viscous black water until they became welded to the mainland.

RÁBIDA ISLAND

The exact geographic center of the Galápagos sits off the southern coast of Santiago. A wet landing drops you onto a rust-colored beach filled with dozens of sea lions stretched out moaning and snoring as if it were the morning after the world's biggest sea-lion party. As you make your way down to the section of beach with grains the size and texture of Grape Nuts cereal, you'll come upon a colony of brown pelicans nesting in the salt bushes. Pelican chicks have a mortality rate of 60–70 percent during their first year of life; hence the numerous corpses scattering the sand. The live ones more than make up the difference, though, filling the air with their pterodactyl-like cries for food.

A salt pond on the other side of the bushes provides food for Galápagos flamingos and yellow-crowned night herons. It's a good spot to find a Galápagos hawk perched on a tree branch, stoically watching the assemblage of young and old sea lions who have claimed the shores of the lagoon as a combination nursery and retirement colony. Newborn pups suckle loudly and bleat for more between rolls in the shallow mud.

The snorkeling near the landing is excellent—just watch out for male sea lions. From here, a trail leads up and over the hillside for a view of the salt pond and the steep cliffs on the other side of the spit. If you're visiting during the dry season, notice how the palo santo trees on the far hillside turn vaguely green at mist level, about halfway up.

SOMBRERO CHINO

The aptly named "Chinese Hat" island, off the east end of Santiago just south of Bartolomé, is open only to boats carrying 12 people or fewer. A wet landing onto a rough coral beach begins a short walk through a broken volcanic landscape, ending above the ocean on the far side. The snorkeling off Sombrero Chino is excellent—just watch the strong current.

Western Islands

Isabela and Fernandina, the largest and least disturbed islands in the Galápagos, respectively, are on most week-long itineraries. A double feature of Tagus Cove and Punta Espinosa makes for an unforgettable day of touring.

ISABELA ISLAND

The largest island in the Galápagos consists of five different volcanoes joined together over the eons by repeated lava flows. From north to south, they are: Wolf (1,646 meters), Darwin (1,280 meters), Alcedo (1,097 meters), Sierra Negra (1,490 meters), and Cerro Azul (1,250 meters), and all remain at least partially active. The 130-kilometer-long island harbors a wide range of habitats and a correspondingly large variety of animal species. It fits most people's mental image of a Pacific island: palm trees, pure white beaches, rocky cliffs, mangroves, and an easy pace of life in the settlements that's interrupted by few tourists. About 1,500 people live on the island, mostly in Puerto Villamil.

Isabela's moist higher altitudes provide an ideal habitat for giant tortoises, and five separate subspecies of tortoise have evolved here, one on each volcano. Volcán Alcedo is home to the most—more than 35 percent of all the tortoises in the archipelago—and Darwin and Wolf together shelter another 15 percent. The cool upwelling waters off Isabela's west coast wash in enough nutrients to support large populations of flightless cormorants and Galápagos penguins, with whales and dolphins common offshore. With so much food available, Isabela's marine iguanas are the largest in the Galápagos.

Some of Isabela's older tortoises have seen the deadly days of the whalers replaced by modern threats. Feral goats, once the plague to tortoises and iguanas, have finally been eradicated, a monstrous task that never received the accolades it deserved. In 1984, an accidental fire on Sierra Negra raged for five months and destroyed much of the volcano's tortoise habitat.

History

Isabela's traffic began arriving in the 18th century, when whalers plied the rich waters to the west, stopping off to gather a few hundred tortoises along the way. The names of some of these ships are still etched into the rocks at Tagus Cove.

In 1946, a penal colony was built on the Sierra Negra's southern slopes, a brutal place filled with the worst offenders from the mainland. Hours were spent on pointless, dangerous tasks to fill the time: The lava-rock *muro de las lagrimas* (wall of tears), still standing near Puerto Villamil, was stacked by countless hands in the hot sun.

Many prisoners are thought to have died at the hands of guards, although the truth may never be known. It's said that one police chief reported to a navy officer, upon receipt of a month's supplies: "Commander, nothing to report. Thirty prisoners fewer." The notorious jail was closed in 1959 after numerous escape attempts and campaigns by local residents to shut it down.

© JEAN BROWN

Normally teeming with birds, the lagoon at Villamil is deserted in the late afternoon.

Puerto Villamil

About 1,500 people live in this settlement on the southern slope of the Sierra Negra Volcano. Various projects have kept the local populace busy since the towns were founded at the turn of the 19th century, including sulfur mining, lime production, coffee farming, and fishing. The tourist infrastructure here is still basic, but those who visit can enjoy the area's beautiful beaches, bird-filled lagoons, and highland hikes.

Isabela Tours (tel. 5/252-9207) is on the plaza and can arrange day trips. Antonio Gil, at the Hotel San Vicente, is one of several people who arranges highland tours ($45 pp). Travel by van to the highlands, then horse-ride to the volcano and hike into the crater. It's a half-hour walk into the uplands west of town to reach the **Centro de Crianza** (La Galapaguera), where Galápagos tortoises are being bred and repopulated to their original areas. Fifteen minutes farther out by car is the *muro de las lagrimas,* in the remains of the penal colony. The **beaches** west of town are good for surfing, and you can snorkel among the mangroves and rocky inlets east of town.

Budget rooms can be found at **San Vicente** (Cormorant and Las Escalacias, tel. 5/252-9140, $23 pp), with breakfast, private bath,

air-conditioning, and hot water. It's often full of groups, and the restaurant offers set meals for $6. **Tero Real** (Tero Real and Opuntia, tel. 5/252-9195) has six cabins with private bath, fans, and refrigerators for $15 s, $20 d. Meals are available at both on request. The lovely new **Albermarle** is on the beach facing the pier. Rooms are $122 s or d, including tax and breakfast on the terrace, and the British owner personally meets his guests.

At the east end of town was the Hotel Ballena Azul, which has just changed hands and was being remodeled as of May 2008. Upon completion, the six double cabins on the beach will have a deck and an outdoor cooking area facing the ocean. It will join the Red Mangrove chain with a new name, **Red Mangrove Sierra** (tel. 5/252-9238, www.redmangrove.com), and prices will be $100 d, including breakfast.

Just a few doors down is **La Casa de Marita** (tel./fax 5/252-9030, info@galapagosisabela .com, www.galapagosisabela.com), a beautiful beachfront place that has seven rooms with kitchenettes, hot water, and private baths for $50 s, $85 d, including breakfast. It also has an elegant family-style restaurant. Keep going a little farther to **Wooden House** (tel. 5/252-9484, www.thewoodenhouse.com), where a

© JEAN BROWN

EMETEBE interisland flights

shady garden and pool invite you to lounge outside. Rooms all have air-conditioning and cable TV and cost $37 pp, including breakfast.

Backpackers should walk to the western end of the village and beyond the bend, where they will find **La Jungla.** Spacious tents with good mattresses can be rented for $5 pp, and small rooms with fans cost $10 pp.

El Encanto de la Pepa is considered the best restaurant in town, with good food in an attractive setting on the plaza. Meals start at $5. On either side, find daily specials at the **La Choza** or the friendly **Yolita.** Enjoy a cold beer out on the pier and watch the surfers on the beach.

The **police station** is on the plaza, and the **National Parks** office is one block away. There is no bank, ATM, or post office—bring cash, because it's next to impossible to change travelers' checks or pay with credit cards here.

Buses leave daily on the 48-kilometer round-trip into the highlands. They depart at 7 A.M. and noon by the market, returning about two hours later. **Trucks** can be rented to spots around town or in the highlands. **EMETEBE** (tel. 5/252-9155) has flights to San

Cristóbal and Baltra for $90–100 pp one way. *Lanchas* (speed boats) sail for Puerto Ayora daily at 6 A.M. from the main dock ($30 pp one-way, three hours).

Isabela Highlands

High above the town of Santo Tomás towers the **Sierra Negra Volcano,** Isabela's oldest and highest. It can be visited in a day trip by horse from Santo Tomás, or a three-to-five-hour hike will bring you to the edge of the huge caldera, 10 kilometers in diameter, where you'll see fumaroles—evidence of the last eruption in 2005. Volcán Chico, another four kilometers away, last erupted in 1979. **Alcedo Volcano,** to the north, has been closed to visitors since 1995. It's recuperating after the goat-eradication program.

Punta Moreno

The first stop here, north of Cerro Azul, is a *panga* ride along the sea cliffs and into a grove of mangroves in search of penguins and great blue herons. Then a three-hour hike takes you from the coast—with its penguins, flightless cormorants, and marine iguanas—to a handful of brackish ponds frequented in season by white-cheeked pintails and flamingos.

Elizabeth Bay

Slightly farther north, in Isabela's elbow, Elizabeth Bay is explored only by *panga*. The scattered islands at the mouth of the bay support small populations of flightless cormorants, penguins, and marine iguanas. A peaceful drift brings you into shallow mangrove lagoons stocked with rays, turtles, and small sharks.

Urbina Bay

In 1954, a volcanic eruption lifted a sizable chunk of seabed six meters above the water's surface so suddenly that a visiting group of scientists found fish still flapping in puddles of seawater. Now visitors can get a slightly surreal look at a coral community, littered with the bones of marine animals and the shells of as many as 30 sea turtles. Flightless cormorants and marine iguanas have moved in already.

Tagus Cove

Centuries of graffiti decorate the rocks above this popular anchorage in the Bolívar Channel, directly across from Fernandina. The older records from whalers and sealers are carved into the rock (one reads 1836), while more recent crews have added the names of their vessels in paint. At three kilometers, this is the longest walk (aside from volcano ascents) in the islands and strenuous in places.

The first 200-meter section above the dry landing follows a steep gully, fragrant with sea-lion droppings, up to the base of a wooden staircase. A short hike beyond the top of the stairs brings **Darwin Lake** into view, filling an eroded crater 12 meters deep in the center. A white ring around the edge is evidence of the lagoon's high salinity, which is too much for most creatures besides the occasional visiting Bahama duck.

Scientists once wondered how the lake filled with water, because it was too saline for

rainwater and too permanent to be filled by the occasional wave washing over the narrow wall between the lake and the bay. The answer? Seawater filters in through porous lava rocks beneath the surface, keeping the water level in the lagoon even with the ocean outside. The small, round pebbles covering the trails began as raindrops that collected airborne volcanic ash and hardened before hitting the ground.

The trail peaks at a lookout over the entire extent of Isabela, including a large lava flow from the Darwin Volcano. Your guide should point out how new plant species began to appear near the top, forming thickets inhabited by the Galápagos flycatcher, finches, and mockingbirds.

A *panga* ride along the cliffs makes up the second half of the visit. Good snorkeling along the rocky northern shore may reward you with close encounters with sea turtles, Galápagos penguins, and sea lions, and handsome noddy terns nest in the caves and shadows. The ocean reaches into the rock itself, forming long caves where you might glimpse the so-called gringo fish—pink on the back, like a sunburned tourist.

FERNANDINA ISLAND

The westernmost island in the Galápagos is one of the most pristine island ecosystems in the world. No foreign species have been introduced, despite heavy traffic nearby during the whaling heyday of the 19th century. Fernandina is many guides' favorite island, and for good reason: if your tour makes it out this far, you'll get to experience a very special place, where a lizard walking across a shattered field of lava seems like a scene from the dawn of time.

Fernandina is the youngest volcanic island in the archipelago (only one million years old), as well as the most active. Eruptions in the wide caldera continued well into the 20th century; one, in 1968, collapsed the entire 30-square-kilometer caldera more than 300 meters. Glowing plumes of lava from a 1991 eruption were captured on videotape by observers.

Our ears were suddenly as-sailed by a sound that could only be equalled by 10,000 thunderers bursting upon the air at once; while the whole hemisphere was lighted up with a horrid glare that might have appalled the stoutest heart.... At the time, the mercury in the thermometer was at 147 [°F], but on immersing it into the water, it instantly rose to 150. Had the winds deserted us here, the consequences must have been horrible.

Benjamin Morrell, describing the 1825 eruption of Fernandina

◖ Punta Espinosa

Fernandina's only visitors site lies on the island's northeast corner across from Isabela's Tagus Cove. After a dry landing in a grove of white mangroves, you'll come to a sandy point that's partly covered by rough lava from recent

flows. The largest colony of marine iguanas in the Galápagos nests nearby, sneezing like the cold ward in a hospital. As you proceed single-file down the beach (to avoid stepping on buried nests), you'll see shells and bleached mangrove trunks littering the sand, evidence of recent volcanic uplifts.

Sea lions fill the pools among the jagged rocks, females and pups playing while males patrol. At the tip of the point waits the highlight: the flightless cormorant nesting site. Each nest—a ragged witch's mop of seaweed and twigs—supports a female sitting regally while her mate hunts for fish. Keep your eyes open for returning males, who offer a seaborne trinket to the female before drying their stubby wings in the ocean breeze.

Back near the landing site. you'll take a detour over the jagged lava, spotted with short, squat *brachycereus* lava cacti. Brilliant vermillion flycatchers often sit in the mangrove branches. A *panga* ride out into the straights where the Cromwell current upwells may reward you with sightings of the strange deepwater sunfish or a school of dolphins.

Southern Islands

South of Santa Cruz, the main attraction of Floreana is its fascinating history. Other highlights include checking your mail at Post Office Bay, snorkeling around the "Devil's Crown," and spotting sea-turtle hatchlings at Punta Cormorant. Punta Suárez on Española is widely considered one of the top visitors sites in the islands.

FLOREANA ISLAND

Floreana's turgid story begins in the 18th century, when the island was bequeathed to an Ecuadorian officer as a reward for bravery in battle. The officer soon held the island's 80 residents in a state of near-slavery, using giant mastiffs as police and bodyguards. An island-wide rebellion eventually forced the Dog King of Charles Island to flee to the mainland.

Life on Floreana got really interesting in the early 20th century. William Beebe's book *Galápagos: World's End* captured the imagination of readers everywhere, particularly in Europe, with its portrayal of the islands as a strangely beautiful "lost paradise." Among these readers were Dr. Friedrich Ritter, a holistic doctor and philosopher, and his lover Dora Strauch, a former patient left crippled by multiple sclerosis. In 1929, the starry-eyed couple left their native Germany and respective spouses to start a new, natural, naked life in the Galápagos.

Ritter and Strauch chose Floreana for its reliable water supply and relatively rich soil, and they named their settlement Friedo, a contraction of their first names. Ritter's accounts of gardening and nudism in the exotic islands

marine iguanas and Sally lightfoot crab

caused a stir when published back in Germany, and the island began to attract passing yachters and more settlers. Friction between the couple began early, though, as Ritter's cold personality and misogynistic Nietzschean philosophy began to wear on his no-longer-blushing bride.

Three years later, the Wittmer family arrived: father Heinz, pregnant wife Margaret, and their 12-year-old son, Harry. Although inspired to come by Ritter's articles, the staunch German family kept to themselves. Later that same year (1932), the most colorful immigrants yet arrived: Eloise Wagner de Bosquet, a self-styled "baroness" with a shady past, along with her two companions, Rudolf Lorenz and Robert Philipsson. Straight out of an S&M fantasy—complete with black boots, crop, riding britches, and pearl-handled revolver— the baroness settled her enclave in Post Office Bay, where she began causing trouble almost at once.

From the start, the baroness acted as if the entire island belonged to her, even to the point of bathing in the main water source, a large cistern near Post Office Bay. She talked of plans to build a luxury hotel on the island while rifling through mail and supplies intended for the Wittmers and Ritter and Strauch. Her relationship with Lorenz and Philipsson was the subject of much speculation. Other residents began to see her as a vindictive, manipulative sex maniac who tormented her "love slaves" for the sheer fun of it. Lorenz began to show signs of physical abuse at the hands of the baroness and Philipsson, and Ritter and Strauch's relationship continued to sour.

By now, the inhabitants of Floreana were known around the world, and luxury yachts stopped by regularly to visit and deliver mail and supplies. A severe drought in March 1934, with temperatures soaring to 50°C, pushed things over the edge. One afternoon, the baroness and Philipsson suddenly left by boat, saying only that they were headed for Tahiti, as if the island were next door instead of halfway across the Pacific. Almost all of their possessions were left behind in the abrupt departure, including the baroness's beloved copy of *The Portrait of Dorian Gray,* sitting on a night table. The pair were never seen again.

Eyebrows lifted during a search of the baroness's house when Ritter allegedly commented, "She won't return. You have my word on it." Lorenz also began exhibiting an ominous new calm, wandering off alone and breaking into abrupt fits of crying for no apparent reason. In July 1934, he left the islands aboard the small boat *Dinamita*, bound for Guayaquil. Within weeks, the boat was reported missing.

Six months later, Ritter—supposedly a vegetarian—became gravely ill from eating spoiled chicken cooked by Strauch. Later, Margaret Wittmer recalled how he cursed Dora with his dying breath, trying to kick her when she approached his bedside. That same month, the mummified bodies of Lorenz and the captain of the *Dinamita* were found on the parched beach of Marchena Island, dead of thirst and starvation. Lorenz's desiccated corpse weighed less than 10 kilograms.

Theories still simmer about what exactly happened among Floreana's unlucky colonizers. Dora Strauch returned to Germany, where she lived until 1942. The Wittmers alone remained to tell the tale. Margaret died at 95 in 2000, leaving the mysteries unsolved, and her descendants still live in Puerto Velasco Ibarra and operate a small guesthouse. Margaret's son Harry was killed in a boating accident in 1951, but her other son, Rolf, the first native resident of the Galápagos, opened a successful tour company that still runs ships around the islands.

Several books tell the story of Floreana, including Margaret's own *Floreana, Isle of the Black Cats* and *Curse of the Giant Tortoise*.

Puerto Velasco Ibarra

A dry pier landing welcomes you to this unofficial visitors site, a small settlement of 80 inhabitants near the original infamous colony. Floreana's isolation makes it ideal for anyone looking to escape the outside world, and agony for anyone addicted to a fast pace of life. There aren't any banks, the electricity is on for just part of the day, and the only mail service is through the Post Office Bay barrel. On top of that, there's only one phone on the island, at the **Pensión Wittmer** (tel. 5/252-0150 or 5/252-1026). Rooms and bungalows all overlook the beach and cost $30 s, $50 d, with fans,

private baths, and hot water. Three meals are $20 more pp.

Buses leave for the highlands early every morning. It's a half-hour drive or a three-hour walk eight kilometers into the highlands to the **Asilo de la Paz,** the island's only water source. Since most of the three-day dive trips out of Puerto Ayora stop here, it may be possible to find passage on one back to Santa Cruz.

Punta Cormorant

After a wet landing at Punta Cormorant, you'll set foot on a beach with a noticeably greenish tinge. Take a closer look, and you'll see bits of olivine, a volcanic material, mixed with the dark sand. From here, a trail leads up and over the neck of the point. Along the way, you'll stop at an overlook above a brackish inland lagoon populated by occasional flamingos and other wading birds, such as white-cheeked pintails, stilts, and gallinules. Floreana's environment, slightly less forbidding than other islands its size, encourages several endemic plants. Along this trail, you might happen across the velvet daisy *(Scalesia villosa)* or the cut-leaf daisy *(Lecocarpus pinnatifidus).*

At the end of the trail awaits the so-called organic beach, covered with an incredibly fine white sand straight out of a Caribbean advertising executive's dream. Powdery enough for an hourglass, the sand is said to be a byproduct of marine life nibbling away at coral (although some scientists disagree). Stingrays and spotted eagle rays are common near the beach, so shuffle your feet if you walk in the water, which is stained the color of cream by the flourlike sand. Sea turtles nest here November–February, but you might see a confused hatchling struggling toward the ocean even in the off-season. Bleached driftwood and the green vines of beach morning glory make this the most beautiful beach on the islands.

Post Office Bay

The practice of leaving mail in a barrel began in 1793, when ships bound for the Pacific whaling grounds would leave letters here to be picked up by homeward-bound ships whose crews would deliver the mail by hand. Today, the barrel has evolved into a wooden box on a pole surrounded by a fascinating assortment of junk: driftwood, bones, T-shirts, business cards, luggage tags, even email addresses scratched into the wood. Tradition dictates that if you find a letter addressed to someone near where you live, you're supposed to take it home with you and deliver it in person. Feel free to leave a postcard or letter yourself (no postage is necessary).

Just a few meters beyond the barrel are a lava tunnel and the rusted remains of a Norwegian fish operation dating to the 1920s.

Corona del Diablo

Actually a marine visitor site, the Devil's Crown is the unmistakable circle of jagged rocks situated offshore from Post Office Bay. The nooks and crannies of the forbidding islet offer great snorkeling, either outside the ring or in the shallow inner chamber, which is reached through a side opening or an underwater arch.

Sea lions and the occasional hammerhead make things interesting from time to time, but you'll almost definitely see colorful tropical species like parrotfish, angelfish, and damselfish. The current on the seaward side can be strong and the water cold.

ESPAÑOLA ISLAND

The southernmost island in the Galápagos is also one of the oldest, weathered down until it pokes just above sea level. It's often the first stop for tours leaving from San Cristóbal, and what an introduction—many different seabirds use the island as a stopover or nesting site. The visitors sites can be crowded, because the island is within reach of day tours from San Cristóbal.

Gardener Bay

A wet landing deposits you on this beautiful, one-kilometer-long crescent beach on the northeast side of Española. While the site is a bit mundane—no hikes, just beach—the snorkeling is excellent. Some of the dozens of sea

© JEAN BROWN

resting after a morning of fishing

lions sprawled on the sand might join you in the water, along with the occasional stingray or white-tipped shark. The beach is an important nesting site for marine turtles, so you might be lucky enough to come across one in the process. Turtle Rock, a short *panga* ride offshore, shelters legions of bright topical fish like moorish idols, damselfish, and parrotfish.

Landlubbers can follow the guide's example and relax or read a book. Notice the endemic Hood mockingbirds, inquisitive little buggers often found squabbling over territory on the beach. In this type of behavior, rare in land birds, two family groups face each other down over an invisible line in the sand and set about displaying—bending down to the ground with tails spread in the air—and screeching.

◖ Punta Suárez

Almost one hour by boat from Gardener Bay on the western tip of Española waits one of the most outstanding visitors sites in the Galápagos. After a wet landing, you'll head out on a trail that loops toward cliffs on the south side of the point. Along the way, you can't miss Boobieville, a major blue-footed booby colony. In fact, you'll have to be careful not to step on any of the nests, parents, or young that sit in the middle of the trail like feathery toll attendants. Guano-stained rocks as far as the eye can see are peppered with boobies in all stages of life, from fuzzy

newborns to mangy-looking teenage equivalents (adolescence is kind to no beast). Everyone who's not a parent is demanding to be fed.

Farther along the trail nest almost all of the waved albatrosses on the globe. Between April and November, about 10,000 breeding pairs nest on Punta Suárez, one of only two breeding sites in the world. (The other is the Isla de la Plata off mainland Ecuador.) You might even be lucky enough to see the elaborate courtship dance, or at least hear the bill-clattering from behind a bush. You'll almost surely witness take-offs and landings, worth a wince or two at best. The soaring giants aren't all that graceful within range of the earth, making landings more an exercise in quick braking and luck. The nearby cliff face makes take-offs a little easier—the birds simply inch to the edge and leap.

Many other seabirds soar over the impressive cliffs at the end of the loop, including the Galápagos hawk, Galápagos dove, and swallow-tailed gulls. Down below, a blowhole sends spray 50 feet into the air with every crashing wave. Española's male marine iguanas, spread on the rocks at the base of the cliffs, boast brighter mating colors than anywhere else in the Galápagos. Neon turquoise spreads over their back and front legs, thought to be the result of eating algae particular to this island. Scientists also hypothesize that they may be a separate species.

Northern Islands

Since they're relatively far from the rest of the archipelago—most boats need an overnight voyage to reach them—the northernmost islands of the Galápagos are visited less frequently. Scuba divers would be foolish to forgo the crossing, though, as Wolf and Darwin Islands are considered "dive-before-you-die" kinds of places.

GENOVESA

Genovesa, also known as Tower Island, provides a jumping-off point for seabirds in the far northeast corner of the archipelago. It's eight hours by boat from its larger neighbors, meaning that the long, rolling crossing is usually done at night (stock up on seasickness remedies). The collapsed caldera that forms the low island opens to the sea to the south—boat captains navigate the tricky entrance to Darwin Bay by lining up the metal towers on shore.

Darwin Bay Beach

Keep an eye on the murky shallows on the way to the wet landing, and you can spot white-tipped sharks. Graffiti recording the names of visiting ships decorates the rocks next to the organic beach. Trails from the beach head into the saltbushes filled with the nests of red-footed boobies and frigatebirds. Huge, hapless chicks stare out from the greenery on every side as their parents compete overhead for nest materials and food. Masked boobies and swallow-tailed gulls also nest here, and you may spot a storm petrel or its nemesis, the short-eared owl.

Another branch of the trail leads over rough rocks next to a series of tidal pools. Yellow-crowned night herons sit on the rocks, half-asleep by day, as lava gulls hover above. Notice how soft the opuntia cactus spines have become here, because the plants don't have to defend against anything more dangerous than a bird's nest.

Prince Philip's Steps

Named in honor of a royal visit in the 1960s, this site near the tip of Darwin Bay's eastern arm is limited to boats of 16 people or fewer. First a *panga* ride along the bottom of the cliffs lets you look for frigatebirds and red-billed tropicbirds. Next, a steep-railed stairway takes you to a trail along the top of the cliffs. Masked and red-footed boobies nest near great frigatebirds among the palo santo trees, as storm petrels swoop overhead.

◖ WOLF AND DARWIN ISLANDS

These tiny islands, around 135 miles northwest of the main group, are visited only by diving tours, which endure a full night at sea to experience some of the best diving in the world. Clashing currents beneath unmistakable **Darwin Arch** bring schools of sharks and barracudas past "cleaning stations" where smaller fish nip off parasites. June–November, whale sharks glide by like spotted buses, and geothermal activity makes bubble streams from the ocean floor.

© JULIAN SMITH

Wolf Island

MOON GALÁPAGOS ISLANDS
Avalon Travel
a member of the Perseus Books Group
1700 Fourth Street
Berkeley, CA 94710, USA
www.moon.com

Editor: Annie M. Blakley
Series Manager: Kathryn Ettinger
Copy Editor: Mia Lipman
Graphics Coordinator: Deb Dutcher
Production Coordinator: Lucie Ericksen
Cover Designer: Nicole Schultz
Map Editor: Kevin Anglin
Director of Cartography: Mike Morgenfeld
Cartographers: Chris Markiewicz, Kat Bennett,
    Jon Niemczyk
Proofreaders: Jamie Andrade, Kia Wang

ISBN: 978-1-59880-539-0

Text © 2009 by Julian Smith.
Maps © 2009 by Avalon Travel.
All rights reserved.

ABOUT THE AUTHORS

Julian Smith

"A life has to move or it stagnates." –Beryl Markham

Julian Smith has been writing since he learned to read, and traveling since his first family trip to Cape Cod as a toddler. A pre-college summer in Brazil sparked a love affair with (and in) Latin America, fueled by a stint studying the cloudforests of Costa Rica. Days after wrangling a degree in biology from the University of Virginia, he found himself hopelessly entangled in a self-publishing venture that resulted nine months later in the one-pound, eight-ounce *On Your Own in El Salvador*, the first in-depth guide to the country.

Moon Ecuador came two years later, inspired by a trip the length of the country in 1996. Since then, he's made many friends in the country as well as climbed Cotopaxi and dived off the Galápagos Islands, which he counts among the most incredible places he's ever been.

He has contributed to *Outside* magazine, the *Washington Post, Los Angeles Times, National Geographic Traveler, New Mexico Magazine, Road Trip USA, Online Travel Planning for Dummies*, and other publications. His *Moon Four Corners* won the Society of American Travel Writers' Lowell Thomas Award for best guidebook in 2004. He also managed to earn a master's degree in wildlife ecology along the way, studying grizzly bear tourism on the coast of British Columbia.

As far as normal jobs go, Julian has done pretty well. He's worked as a Canyonlands National Park ranger, guided tourists through the Central American rainforest, and tried (in vain) to protect the vegetable garden of one of the richest men in the world from marauding rodents. Along the way he's found himself freezing atop Kilimanjaro, meditating in a Japanese Zen temple, doused with rum in a Cuban Santería ceremony, and fleeing from Ugandan pygmies, through absolutely no fault of his own.

He currently lives in Santa Fe, NM, where he gets outside as much as humanly possible. For more travel writing, photography, and assorted oddities, stop by his website, www.juliansmith.com.

Jean Brown

Jean Brown was born in London and raised in a small village in Hertfordshire. In school, she studied map-making and was fascinated by geography. To this day she carries scores of maps in her head.

Jean went on to study at Liverpool College of Art before completing a teaching qualification, all the while traveling throughout Western Europe. Inspired by the many tales of her fellow student travelers, Jean set out for South America, where she taught ESL with the English Teaching Theatre in Brazil. She participated in televised English classes, becoming a minor celebrity in southern Brazil in her mid-twenties.

Shortly after, Jean found her home in the Andes. After thirteen rewarding years in education, she moved to the Ecuadorian coast to run the Salango Archaeological Study Center. She continued to travel extensively, exploring the length and breadth of the country and seeking out most of the lesser-known hot springs. Some of her most memorable adventures include paddling down the Shiripuno River in a dugout canoe with a dozen Huaorani Indians, as well as her very first kayaking lesson, where she ended up swimming after her kayak in a Class Three river.

Her extensive knowledge of Ecuador eventually placed her in the travel business. Based in Quito, Jean has been a part of Safari Tours for sixteen years. She frequently surprises locals with her knowledge of the country, and has been referred to as "a walking encyclopedia of Ecuador." Her office often resembles a social club, full of people sharing new information and tales of their travels.